Botanical Names of the Wild Flowers. What They Mean. How Pronounced

BOTANICAL NAMES OF THE WILD FLOWERS

What they mean. How Pronounced.

Botanical Names of the Wild Flowers

What they mean. How Pronounced.

By

Colonel J. S. F. Mackenzie

Author of " Wild Flowers and how to name them at a glance,"
" British Orchids : how to tell one from another," etc.

London
Holden & Hardingham Ltd.
Adelphi

PREFACE

MANY of us, no doubt, are prevented trying to learn the names of the Wild Flowers we see in our lanes and meadows because of the uncouth look of their botanical names.

We are uncertain as to how these barbarous words ought to be pronounced; we know not what their so-called " scientific " names mean.

The Greek or Latin names given to Wild Flowers are not, in themselves, in any way " scientific." These words were those in common everyday use by the Greeks or Latins when the flower first happened to be named.

If Chrysanthemum were scientific, so also would Goldilocks be. Both have practically the same meaning.

Chrysanthemum is a compound Greek word, "chrys" —golden, "anthos,"—flower; Goldilocks, a compound English word and the common name for the Wood Crowfoot, is nothing more than a translation of its second Latin botanical name " auricomus," " auri "— golden, " comus "—hair or locks.

But there is a very great advantage in using the botanical name. By so doing we are using a " standardized " name. By it every one all over the

world knows exactly the plant referred to.   It is other-
wise if we use the Common English name.   This often
varies in different parts of the country.   The plant
botanically known as Galium Aparine has the popular
English names of Goosegrass, Cleavers, or Catchweed.
Some know it under one name, some under another.
Once I have heard it called " Scratch Tongue."   On
asking why such a name, I was told that boys were in
the habit of putting out their tongue and scratching it
with the leaf to see whose tongue would bleed most.

On the other hand, the popular English names, in
spite of the confusion which arises from the same plant
being known by a different name in a different part of
the country, are full of meaning, and much more
interesting.   " Scratch Tongue," when you know how
it came by its name, is much more likely to stick in
your brain than " Galium Aparine," even when you
know what these Latin and Greek words mean.

To Linneus, the great Swedish botanist, and founder
of modern botany, belongs the honour and glory of
having evolved a scientific plan for the naming of Wild
Flowers.

When Linneus lived—born in 1707, died 1778—Latin
was the universal language commonly used by writers
of all countries.   He therefore wrote in Latin, and gave
to plants the Latin names by which they were known
to the ancients.

Linneus' plan is as simple as it is efficient.   To every
plant he gave two names, and no two plants have
exactly the same two names.   The first or group name
corresponds to the surname of human beings.   All
plants botanically alike, or, so to say, belonging to one
and the same household, is given a group name.   This

group name is peculiar to, and only given to the members of the same household.

Some groups have many members, some only one.

According to Bentham and Hooker's " British Flora " (6th Ed.), Wild Flowers are divided into 501 groups.

Although we have so many group names, no two have the same name. Several are somewhat alike, but yet are different.

We have the same sort of thing with our surnames. Smith and Smythe are alike, but yet are different.

The second Botanical Name corresponds to the Christian name of human beings, and like that, enables us to distinguish the different individuals of the same household.

The same second botanical name can *not* be given to two members of the same group.

But the same second botanical name is found in many different groups.

Usually these second botanical names indicate some characteristic of the plant, as " hirsutus "—hairy, " latifolia "—broadleaved, &c.; or tell us where they are to be found, as " arvensis "—a cultivated field, " sylvestris "—a wood or shady place, &c.

There is one not uncommon—for it is found in several groups—second botanical name " officinalis." This means " belonging to the shop." It not only distinguishes the individual, but it gives us more information. It tells that the plant is one of those in whose medicinal virtues our fathers firmly believed, and that herbalists—the chemists of those days—kept in their shops a stock of the plant to meet the constant demand.

Thus it will be seen the plan is very simple. Every

plant has two names. One a surname, the other a Christian name, so to say. But the combination of the two names can only be given to one plant wherever it may be found.

You can have any number of, so to say, Johns, or Edwards, &c. To follow the botanical method of putting the surname first, you can have Smith John, Mackenzie John, &c., or Peterson Edward, or Morgan Edward, or &c.; but throughout the whole land you cannot have two Smith John or two Morgan Edward, &c.

Result: each plant has its own peculiar name, applicable only to itself.

When one realizes that the botanical names are simple words, full of meaning; only they are in Latin dress instead of English, their forbidding look seems to melt away, and they stick in one's memory more easily.

Groups, which from a botanist's point of view are related, are in their turn grouped into Families.

There are 94 families in all; each contains a varying number of groups. Some families have only one group, while the Composite Family has 41.

The family name is generally obtained by adding the Latin termination " aceus "—like to the name of the most important group contained in the family. Thus " Rosaceae "—" Rosa " and " aceus "—is the name of a family containing 16 groups, of which Rosa, being the most important, it gives its name to the family.

It is impossible now, with any certainty, to determine how plants came by their names. We must be content to accept the most reasonable guess.

Several of the group names are, by way of honouring

them, merely the names of famous botanists slightly altered to make them look like Latin words. For example, "Bartsia," the name for a group is named after John Bartsch, a Dutch botanist, who died in 1736. Only one lady is among those so honoured, and she was an Irish botanist, Miss Hutchins. The group " Hutchinsia " is so named after her.

Alcock, in his most interesting work, "Botanical Names for English Readers," tells us that, according to Pliny, " Polemonium," the Greek and Latin name for Greek Valerian or Jacob's Ladder, was derived from " polemos "—war, the plant having caused a war between two Kings, who each of them claimed its discovery. Another derivation is that it was so named after Polemon, a King of Pontus, who died 270 years before Christ.

It is immaterial now which derivation is correct. They both, together with the fact that many plants were named after their gods, goddesses, heroes or eminent men, sufficiently prove that the ancients set a high value on the discovery of the medical properties of plants.

J. S. F. MACKENZIE.

ABBREVIATIONS.

A.S.   for   Anglo-Saxon.
Eng.   ,,   English.
G.   ,,   Greek.
L.   ,,   Latin.
adj.   ,,   adjective.
bot.   ,,   botanical.
dim.   ,,   diminutive.

BOTANICAL NAMES OF THE WILD FLOWERS

WHAT THEY MEAN. HOW PRONOUNCED.

A

Abele (a-be-le). Polish. " Bialo " (white) ; a name for the White Poplar.

Aberrant (ab-er-rant). L. " Aberro " (going astray) ; differing from the usual structure.

Abies (ab-i-es). L. name for Fir tree.

Abrupt (ab-rupt). L. " Ab " (from), " rumpo " (to break) ; suddenly ending as if broken off.

Absinthium (ab-sin-thi-um). L. name for Wormwood, which gives the well-known French liqueur—absinth—its peculiar flavour.

Acacia (a-ka-shi-a). G. " Akakia " (a thorn); name for the Egyptian thorn, from which tree gum-arabic is obtained.

Acanthium (a-kan-thi-um). G. " Akantha " (a fine thorn). Acanthium was the G. name for the plant imitated on the Corinthian capitals.

Acanthoides (a-kan-thoi-dez). G. " Akantha " (a thorn); " oides " (like) ; i.e., thorny.

Acaulous (a-kaw-lus). G. " A " (no); "kaulos " (stem); refers to a feature of the plant.

Acaulescent (a-kaw-les-sent). Somewhat without a stem.

Accrescent (ak-kres-ent). L. Adj. growing after flowering.

Acuminate (a-ku-mi-nat). To narrow to a tapering point.

Acuminatus (a-ku-mi-na-tus). L. "Acumen" (a point); adj. pointed.

Acutus (a-ku-tus). L. adj., sharp pointed.

Acutifolium (a-ku-ti-fo-li-um). L. "Acuti" (pointed); "folium" (leaf); the plant having pointed leaves.

Adder's-Tongue. The English translation of the bot. name of the group Ophioglossum.

Adiantum (ad-i-an-tum). G. name for the Maidenhair Fern. Takes its name, "a" (not), "diantos" (moistened), because it was thought that even if placed in water it would not get wet. Bot. name for Maidenhair group.

Adonis (a-do-nis). Name of a G. youth, one of Venus' lovers, whose blood stained the petals of the flower Pheasant's Eye. Said to be the only pure crimson wild flower. Bot. name of a group.

Adoxa (a-doks-a). G. "A" (no); "doxa" (glory); refers to the humble growth of the plant. Bot. name for Moschatel group.

Adpressa (ad-pres-sa). L. "Ad" (to); "pressus" (pressed); from the pods being close to, touching, but not united to the stem.

Adustus (a-dust-us). L. adj. From "aduro" (I burn); burnt up; scorched.

Adscitus (ad-si-tus). L. adj. "Ad" (to); "scitus" (known); known to be true.

Ægopodium (a-go-po-di-um). G. "Aigos" (a goat); "podium" (foot); from some fancied resemblance of the leaf to a goat's-foot. Bot. name Goutweed group.

Æmuluem (em-u-lum). L. adj., vying with.

Æstvum (es-te-vum).

Æstivalis (es-ti-val-is). Both from L. " æstivus " (summertime); when the flower blooms.

Æstivation (es-ti-va-shion). The arrangement of leaves of flower-bud, which bursts into flower in summer.

Æthusa (ae-thu-sa). G. " Aetho " (to burn); from the acridity of the plant. Bot. name, Fool's Parsley group.

Affinis (af-fin-is). L. adj., bordering on, or related to.

Aggregatum (ag-gre-gat-um). L. Primarily " to bring into the flock," hence to add to.

Agraphis, (a-graf-is). G. " A " (no); " graphis " (writing); because the petals had no writing-like marks upon them as is the case in some other hyacinths.

Agraria (ag-ra-ri-a). L. " Ager " (a field); hence belonging to the land.

Agrestis (ag-res-tis).

Agrestinum (ag-res-ti-num). Both from L. " ager " (a field, or countrified); hence wild.

Agrimonia (ag-re-mo-ni-a). G. name for " pearl in the eye." The plant was supposed to be a cure for cataract of the eye. Bot. name of Agrimony group.

Agrimony (ag-re-mo-ne). The English rendering of Agrimonia.

Agropyrum (ag-ro-pi-um). G. " Agro " (wild); " pyrum " (wheat); allied to the parents of the cultivated wheats. Bot. name for a group.

Agrostemma (ag-ros-tem-ma). G. " Agro " (fields); " stemma " (crown); hence crown of the fields. Some botanists use this word as a group name for a subdivision of Lychnis group.

Agrostis (ag-ros-tis). G. " Agros " (belonging to the country); hence wild. Bot. name for a group.

Aira (ayr-a). G. name for a rank grass that grows in the wheat. The Darnel, which is supposed to be the Tares of Scripture. Bot. name for a group.

Aizoides (ai-zoi-des). G. " Ai " (ever); " zoon " (living). Second bot. name for one of the Saxifrages.

Ajacis (a-jay-sis). Some marks at the base of the united petals of the Common Larkspur, which have been compared to the letters AIAI, have given rise to the name Ajacis (Bentham & Hooker).

Ajuga (a-ju-ga). Corrupted from " abiga." L. name for a plant used for procuring abortion. Bot. name for the group Bugle.

Ala (a-la). L. " Ala " (a wing). The two outside petals of a pea-shaped flower are winged petals.

Alate (a-late). L. " having wings." Like the appendages of some fruit of trees by which the seed is carried away from the parent.

Alatum (a-la-tum). L. adj., winged.

Alatostyle (a-la-to-stile). L. " Alato " (winged); " style." See STYLE.

Alba (al-ba).

Album (al-bum). Both L. adj., " white." A common second bot. name used for many plants.

Albescent (al-bes-sent).

Albesciens (al-bes-sens). Both L. adj., " whitish."

Albumen (al-bew-men). The substance contained in the seed, and on which, until it has thrown out rootlets, the young plant lives.

Alburnum (al-ber-num). L. " Albus " (white); Sap-

wood., *i.e.*, the soft white part of a tree next to
the bark.

Alchemillia (al-kem-il-lya). Arabic. "Al" (the);
"kimia" (secret art). The plants so named
because much used in Alchemy. Bot. name for
group Alchemil.

Alder (al-der). Corruption of A.S. "aller," name of
the tree. According to Virgil, the first boats were
made of Alder wood.

Alexanders (al-egz-an-der). English name for the
Smyrnium, formerly much used as a pot-herb.
Gets its L. name Alexandrinum, being a plant of
Macedon, Alexander's country.

Algae (al-je). L. for Sea-weed.

Alisma (a-liz-ma). From the Celtic word for water.
Bot. name for the Water Plantain group.

Alismaceae (a-liz-ma-she-a). "Alisma," with L. suffix
"aceus" (like) tacked on, *i.e.*, Alisma-like. Bot.
name Alisma Family.

Alkanet (al-ka-net). Arabic. "Al" (the); "kanah,"
(reed). English name for Anchusa group. Roots
of plant yield a red dye.

Allgood (awl-good). Synonym for Good King Henry.

Allheal (awl-heal). Synonym for Common Valerian.

Alliaria (al-li-ar-ia). Bot. name for group which
includes Garlic Mustard. The leaves of the plant,
when crushed, give off a strong smell of garlic.
Name from L. "allium" (garlic).

Allium (al-li-um). L. name for garlic. Bot. name for
a group, Lily Family.

Allosorus (al-lo-so-rus). G. "Allos" (various);
"soros" (heap); refers to the groups of seed
vessels on the Fern fronds.

Allseed (awl-seed). Eng. name for Radiola group. It is a free translation of the second bot. name.

Alnus (al-nus). L. name for the Alder. Bot. name for this group.

Aloides (al-oi-des). G. " Alo " (the aloe); " oides " (like); aloe-like.

Alopecurus (al-o-pec-u-rus). G. " Alopec " (a fox); " urus " (a tail). Bot. name for the Foxtail group of grasses.

Alpestris (al-pest-ris).

Alpinus (al-pin-us). L. adj., " alpine," from L. " alpes " (high mountain). A very common second bot. name for plants growing on hills.

Alpicola (al-pi-co-la). L. " Alpi " (Alps); " cola " (dweller); *i.e.*, Alpine.

Alsine (al-si-ne). G. name for some unknown plant; used as a synonym for Arenaria by some botanists.

Alsineoides (al-si-noi-des). G. " Alsine " and " oides " (like); alsine-like.

Alsinefolium (al-si-ne-fol-i-um). G. " alsine " and L. " folium " (leaf); alsine-leafed, used as a second bot. name.

Alsike (al-si-ke). Eng. name for Trifolium hybridum.

Alternate (al-ter-nat). When the leaf or flower is first on one side of the stem and the next on the other side.

Alterniflorum (al-ter-ni-flor-um). Flowers on alternate sides.

Alternifolium (al-ter-ni-fo-li-um). L. Leaves on alternate sides.

Altissima (al-tis-si-ma). L. adj., " highest."

Althaea (al-the-a). G. " Altho " (to cure); from its

medicinal qualities. Bot. name group of Mallow family.

Alsinastrum (al-si-nast-rum). The L. termination, "astrum," means like but not the same thing, *i.e.*, Alsine-like.

Alveolate (al-ve-o-late). L. "Alveolus" (a hollow vessel); marked as if honey-combed.

Alyssum (al-is-sum). G. " A " (no); " lyssum " (dog-madness); the plant being a supposed remedy for bite from mad dog. Bot. name for a group.

Amara (a-mar-a). L. adj., " bitter."

Amaranthus (am-ar-anth-us). G. "A" (not); "marian" (dying away); unfading.

Amarella (a-mar-el-la). L. adj., "somewhat bitter "; is the diminutive of L. ",amarus " (bitter).

Amaryllideae (am-a-ril-li-de-a). Bot. name of a family; from Amaryllis, the name of a country girl in Virgil.

Ambigua (am-big-u-a). L. adj., "indefinite."

Amethysta (a-meth-ist-a). G. " A " (not); " methu-ston " (intoxicating); *i.e.*, a violet-blue colour, like wine mixed with water.

Amentiferous (a-men-tif-er-us). L. " Amentum " (a catkin); " ferous " (bearing).

Amentaceæ (a-men-ta-si-a). Bot. name for Catkin family; from " amentum."

Ammophila (am-mo-fil-a). G. "Ammo" (sand); " phila " (loving); because the plant loves a sandy soil.

Amomum (a-mo-mum). L. name for an Indian spice plant, and now used as second bot. name for Bastard Stone Parsley.

Ampeloprasum (am-pel-o-prasum). G. " Ampelos " (a vine); " prasum " (a sea plant); like the leek.

Amphibian (am-fib-i-an). G. "Amphi" (both); "bios" (life); *i.e.*, lives on land or water.

Amphitropeus (am-fit-ro-peus). G. "Amphi" (both); "tropeus" (turning).

Amplexicaulis (am-pleks-i-kawl-is. G. "Amplexi" (embracing); "caulis" (the stem); this is what the leaves of many plants do.

Amplificatus (am-pli-fi-ca-tus). L. adj., enlarging.

Ampullacea (am-pul-la-si-a). L. "Ampulla" (a bottle); hence bottle-shaped or globular.

Amygdalina (a-mig-da-lin-a). L. adj., made of almonds.

Amygdaloides (a-mig-da-loi-des). G. "Amygdale" (an almond); "oides" (like).

Anagallis (an-a-gal-lis). G. "Ana" (again); "gallis" (adorning); refers to the plant springing up year after year in the same place. Bot. name, Pimpernel group.

Anacamptis (an-a-kamp-tis). G. "Anakampti" (to bring back). A herb, probably a stone crop, the touch of which was said to bring back a love that was lost.

Anacardium (an-a-kard-ium). G. "Ana" (like to); "kardia" (a heart). Name of a group of trees, one of which gives cashew or marking nut.

Anacharis (anak-ar-is). G. "Ana" (without); "charis" (beauty).

Anastomose (an-as-to-mose). When the smaller veins of a leaf are connected together like the meshes of a net.

Anatropeus (an-at-ro-pe-us). G. "Ana" (up); "trope" (turning); when the ovule is inverted; *i.e.*, the bottom is at the top and the top is down below.

Anceps (an-seps). L. adj., double sided.

Anchusa (an-chu-sa). G. "Paint" refers to the use of the root as a dye. Bot. name Alkanet group.

Ancipital (an-sip-i-tal). L. adj., double-edged.

Androsaemum (an-dro-say-mum). G. "Andros" (a man); "aima" (blood); refers to blood-like juice of the capsule.

Androecium (an-dre-si-um). G. "Andros" (a man); "oikos" (a house, *i.e.*, all the stamens together).

Androgynous (an-droj-i-nus). G. "Andro" (a man); "gune" (a woman); a spike or head of flowers where male and female flowers are mixed.

Andromeda (an-drom-e-da). After a Grecian Princess, who was bound to a rock whence she was freed by Perseus. Bot. name for a group.

Androphore (an-drof-or-e). G. "Andro" (a man); "phono" (to bear); a stalk supporting the stamen.

Androspores (an-dro-sporz). G. "Andro" (male); "spora" (seed); developed male organs in certain Algae.

Anemone (a-nem-o-ne). G. "Animos" (the wind); because the plant loves the wind. Bot. name for a group.

Anemagrostis (an-e-mag-ros-tis). G. "Animos" (the wind); "agrostis" (name for a special kind of grass on which mules were fed).

Anglicus (ang-gli-cus). L. adj. from Angli, the name of a German tribe; also gives its name to England, *i.e.*, Angle-land.

Angelica (an-jel-ik-a). L. Named after the angels because of the good medical properties and pleasant taste of the plant. Bot. name for a group.

Angiospermous (an-ji-o-sper-mus). G. "Angio" (a

vessel); " sperma " (seeds); plants having their
seeds enclosed in a pod.

Angularis (ang-gu-la-ris). L. adj., having corners.

Angustifolium (an-gust-i-fol-ium). L. " Angustus "
(narrow); " folium " (leaf); narrow-leafed; a very
common second bot. name.

Angustissimus (an-gust-is-si-mus). L. adj., superlative
of " angustus "; narrowest.

Anisomerous (an-i-som-er-us). G. "An" (not); "isos"
(equal); " meros " (parts); unsymmetrical; when
some of the flowers in a whorl have some parts
different from the others.

Aniseed (an-i-seed). The seed of the " anisum," the
G. name for plant.

Annotium (an-not-i-num). L. adj., a year old, of last
year.

Annual (an-nu-al). L. " Annualis " (lasting a year);
a plant that comes up, blooms, and dies all in the
year.

Annular (an-nu-ler). L. " Annulus " (a ring); applied
to any parts of a plant disposed in a circle.

Anserina (an-ser-ina). L. " Anser " (a goose, that
bird being fond of the plant).

Antennaria (an-ten-nar-ia). L. "Antenna " (a sail-
yard); so named because the hairs attached to the
seeds of the plant are like the feelers (called
" antenna " from their sail-yard-like look) of
insects. Bot. name of a group.

Anterior (an-te-ri-or). L. The front or outside.

Anthemis (an-them-is). G. "Anthos " (a flower). The
flower of flowers, because of its great medicinal
properties. Bot. name for Chamomile group.

Anther (an-ther). G. "Antheros" (belonging to a flower); name given to the pollen sac which contains the fertilizing dust of the male flower.

Anthesis (an-the-sis). G. "Antheo" (to bloom); the period of flowering.

Anthocarpus (an-tho-kar-pus). G. "Anthos" (a flower); "karpos" (a fruit); fruit formed from the united seed-vessels of several flowers.

Anthocyane (an-tho-si-an-e). G. "Anthos" (flower); "kuanos" (dark blue); the substance which gives dark blue colour to flowers.

Anthodium (an-tho-dium). G. "Anthos" (flower); "oides" (like); flowery.

Antholites (an-tho-lites). G. "Anthos" (flower); "lithos" (a stone); the impression of fossil flowers found in rocks.

Anthophore (an-tho-for). G. "Anthos" (flower); "phoreo" (to carry); a stalk supporting inner floral envelope and separating them from calyx.

Anthotaxis (an-tho-take-is). G. "Anthos" (flower); "taxis" (arrangement); the manner in which flowers are arranged.

Anthoxanthum (an-tho-zan-thum). G. "Anthos" (flower); "xanthos" (yellow). Bot. name for a group of the grasses.

Anthriscus (an-thris-cus). G. name for the plant; used as its second name.

Anthropophora (an-thro-po-for-a). G. "Anthros" (a man); "phoreo" (to carry). Second bot. name given to the Man Orchis, because the flower is supposed to be like a man.

Anthyllis (an-thil-lis). G. "Anthos" (flower); "ioulos" (a beard); from the down which covers

the cup at the base of flower. Bot. name of one
of the groups.

Anticous (an-ti-kus). L. "Anticus" (in front); placed
in front of flower, like the lip of an orchid.

Antirrhinum (an-ti-ri-num). G. "Anti" (opposite);
"rhina" (the nose); from the mask-like look of the
flower—Snapdragon. Bot. for a group.

Antiquorum (an-tik-or-um). L. "Antiqus" (ancient,
most celebrated).

Antitropal (an-ti-trop-al). G. "Anti" (against);
"tropeo" (turn).

Antrorse (an-trors). L. adj., growing upwards or for-
wards.

Apargia (ap-ar-je-a). G. "Apo" (from); "argia"
(idleness); G. name for unknown plant, and used
by some botanists as bot. name for the Hawkbit
group.

Aparine (ap-ar-ine). G. name for the Goosegrass,
adopted by the Latins and used as second bot. of
the plant.

Apera (a-pera). L. adj., opened.

Apetala (a-pet-ala).

Apetulus (a-pet-u-lus). G. "A" (no); "petalon"
(petal); *i.e.*, both petalless.

Apex (a-peks). A short, sharp, but not stiff point in
which a leaf or other organ ends.

Aphaca (af-ak-a). G. name for some kind of vetch, but
used as second bot. name for Yellow Vetch.

Aphanes (af-an-es). G. "Unseen or unnoticed."
Linneus thought this plant—Parsley Piert—sufficiently distinct to have a group of its own, and
called it Aphanes, but Bentham and Hooker have
included it in Alchemil group.

Aphyllum (af-fil-lum). G. "A" (no); "phullon" (leaf); leafless.

Apiculate (a-pik-u-late). L. Suddenly terminated by a distinct point.

Apifera (a-pi-fera). L. "Apis" (a bee); "fera" (bearer); bee-bearer; the second bot. name for the Bee Orchis, the flower having a resemblance to a bee.

Apium (ap-i-um). L. name for Wild Celery. Bot. name for a group.

Apocarpus (ap-o-kar-pus). G. "Apo" (from); "kar-pus" (fruit); when the seed-vessels are quite separate or only partially united.

Apocynaceæ (apo-sin-a-si-a). G. "Apocynon" (name for Dogsbane, so named because it was fatal to dogs) and L. "aceous" (like), a suffix tacked on. Bot. name for Periwinkle family.

Apopetalous (apo-pet-al-us). G. "Apo" (from); "petalon" (a petal); applied to Corollas, whose petals are distinct and disconnected.

Apophyllous (a-pof-il-us). G. "Apo" (from); "phullon" (a leaf); applied to perianth whose parts are distinct and separate.

Apophysis (a-pof-i-sis). G. "Apo" (from); "phuo" (to grow); an irregular swelling on the surface; a tubercule at the base of the seed-vessels of certain mosses.

Apothecium (a-po-the-shi-um). G. "Apotheke" (a spore); a cluster of spore cells in lichens often cup-shaped.

Appendiculate (ap-pen-dik-ul-at). L. "Appendicula" (a small appendage).

Applanate (ap-plan-at). L. "Ad" (to); "planatus" (made flat); flattened out.

Apple (ap-pl). A.S. "Aepl," name for the well-known fruit.

Appressed (ap-prest). L., "Ap" (to); "pressus" (presses); leaves closely squeezed together but not joined.

Apricot (a-pri-kot). Arabic. "Al" (the); "birouk" peach.

Apryenus (a-pry-en-us). G. "An" (no); "pureen" (seed); fruit which produces no seed, as the seedless orange.

Apterous (ap-ter-us). G. "A" (no); "pteron" (wing); no membranous expansions.

Aquaticus (a-kwat-ik-us.

Aquatilis (a-kwat-il-lis). Both L. adj., "aqua" (water); found or growing in water. A very common second bot. name.

Aquifoliaceæ (a-kwi-fol-ia-shi-e). L. "Aquifoli"— see Aquifolium—and "aceous" (like). Bot. name for the Holly family.

Aquifolium (a-kwi-foli-i-um). L. "Ac" (sharp) ("c" and "qu" interchange); "folium" (leaf); having pointed leaves like the Holly.

Aquilina (a-kwil-in-a). L. adj., "aquila" (an eagle); belonging to the Eagle. Second bot. name for the Bracken.

Aquilegia (a-kwil-e-ji-a). L. "Aquila" (an eagle); because that part of the flower where the honey is to be found was supposed to be like the claws of the eagle. Bot. name for Columbine group.

Arabica (ar-ab-ik-a). The L. form of Arabian.

Arabis (ar-ab-is). So named because the "Rockcress"

is common in Arabia. Bot. name for Rockcress group.

Aracae (a-ras-e). G. Supposed to be derived from an Egyptian word, "ar" (fire); refers to fiery taste of plant.

Arachnoid (a-rak-noyd). G. "Arachne" (a spider); "eidos" (like); cob-web like.

Aralia (a-ra-le-a). An American word for Ivy.

Araliaceæ (a-ra-li-a-si-e). "Aralia" and L. "aceous" (like). Bot. name for Ivy family.

Aranifera (a-ra-nif-er-a). L. "Aranea" (a spider); "fera" (carry). Second bot. for Spider Orchis, because the flower is like a spider.

Araucaria (a-raw-kar-i-a). After an Indian tribe in Chile, where this pine grows.

Arborea (ar-bor-ea).

Arborescent (ar-bor-es-cent). Both L. adj., tree-like; from "arbor" (a tree).

Arbuscula (ar-bus-ku-la). L. "Arbusculus" (a little tree); small tree-like shrubs.

Arbutus (ar-bewt-us). L. name for plant. Bot. name for a group.

Arbutifolia (ar-bewt-i-fol-ia). L. "Arbutus" and folia" (leaves); leaves like those of the Arbutus.

Archangel (ark-an-jel). One of the names of Yellow Archangel; so named because it is in flower on the Archangel St. Michael's day.

Archangelica (ark-an-jel-i-ka). Group name for the cultivated garden Angelica.

Archegonium (ar-ke-go-ni-um). G. "Arche" (beginning); "gone" (generation); the reproductive organs of plants, such as mosses and ferns, whose stamens and pistils are not distinctly visible.

Arctium (ark-ti-um).   G.   " Arktos " (a bear); refers
to the general rough look of the plant. Bot. name,
Burdock group.
Arctostaphylos (ark-to-staf-il-os).   G.   " Arktos " (a
bear; " staphylos " (a bunch of grapes); so called
from the fruit being eaten by bears. Bot. name
Bearberry group.
Arcuata (ar-ku-ata).   L.   " Arcutus " (a bow); bent
like a bow.
Arenaria (ar-en-ar-i-a).   L.   " Arena " (sand); the soil
the plant likes. Bot. name Sandwort group.
Argemone (ar-ge-mo-ne).   G.   " Argos " (slothful);
from the narcotic effects of the Poppy. Second
bot. name Pale Poppy.
Argentea (ar-jent-ea).   L. adj., silvery; from the silvery
look of the under side of the leaves.
Aria (a-ri-a).   G. name for some kind of Oak.
Aril (ar-il).
Arillus (ar-il-us).   In some plants, after the egg is
fertilized, the stalk by which the seed is attached
to the inside of the ovary swells up and covers the
seed, more or less, with a pulpy substance called
Aril or Arillus, as is the case with the seed of the
Yew.
Aristatum (a-ris-ta-tum).   L. adj., having ears like
corn.
Aristolochiaceæ (ar-is-to-lo-ki-a-se-e).   G.   " Arito-
lochia " (name of a plant promoting childbirth);
and L. suffix " aceus " (like). Bot. name for one
of the families.
Armeria (ar-mer-i-a).   Said to be derived from the
French " armoires." Now used as bot. name for
Thrift group.

Armoracia (ar-mor-ak-ia). Celtic. "Ar" (on) "mor" (se); on the seashore. Armorica was the old name for Brittany, France, where the Horse Radish grew in abundance.

Arnica (ar-ni-ka). G. "Arnion" (a little lamb); from the leaf being like the soft coat of a lamb; sometimes called Mountain Tobacco; formerly enjoyed some repute as a stimulant in paralytic affections.

Arnoseris (ar-no-ser-is). G. "Arnos" (a lamb); "seris" (chicory). Bot. name for a group.

Arnott (ar-not).

Arnut (ar-nut). A.S. Both contracted forms of "earth-nut."

Arnotto (ar-not-to). A corrupted West Indian word. It is the reddish pulp covering of a seed, and is used to colour cheese and butter. Sometimes spelt Annoto.

Aroideæ (a-roid-e). G. "Aron"—see Arum; "oides" (like). Bot. name Arum family.

Aromaticus (a-ro-mat-i-kus). L. "Aroma" (spice); aromatic.

Arrhenatherum (ar-hen-a-ther-um). G. "Arrhen" (a male); "ather" (an awn). Bot. name for False-Oat group.

Arrow Grass. Eng. name for the Triglochin group.

Arrow Head. Eng. name for the Sagittaria group.

Artemisia (ar-te-miz-i-a). After Artemis, one of the names of Diana, to whom the plant was dedicated. Wormwood.

Arthrolobium (ar-thro-lo-bi-um). G. "Arthros" (a joint); "lobos" (a pod). In their (Bentham & Hooker) first edition the Sand Bird's-foot was

placed in a group of this name; now it is included
in the Bird's-foot group.

Articulatus (ar-tik-u-la-tŭs). L. adj., jointed.

Arum (a-rum). G. "Aron" (the name of the plant).
Said to be derived from an Egyptian word, "ar"
(fire); refers to fiery taste of the plant. Bot. name
for a group.

Arundinacea (a-run-di-na-she-a). L. "Arundo" (a
reed); and "aceus" (like); i.e., reedlike.

Arundo (a-run-do). L. "Arundo" (a reed). Bot.
name for Reed group.

Arvalis (ar-val-is).

Arvensis (ar-ven-sis). Both from L. "arvum" (a
field); refers to cultivated fields, where the plant
is to be found. A common second name for many
plants.

Asafœtida (as-a-fet-da). L. "Asa" (gum); "foetida"
(fetid); a gum resin having a highly offensive smell,
much used in medicine.

Asarabacca (as-a-ra-bak-a). Suppose it must be classed
as the Eng. (?) name for the Asarum. L.
"Asarum" (wild spikenard); "bacca" (a berry).

Asarum (a-sar-um). G. "A" (not); "seria" (a
wreath); because the plant was never used in
wreaths. Bot. name for a group.

Ascendens (as-send-ens). L. adj., growing upwards.
Stems are said to be ascending or "decumbent"
when they spread horizontally at base and then turn
and become erect.

Ascidia (as-sid-i-a). G. "Askidion" (a little bag); a
form of leaf in which the stalk is hollowed out and
closed by the blade as if it were a lid, Pitcher plant.

Asepalous (a-sep-al-us). G. "A" (no); "sepal"

(a leaf); the "pet" in petalon (G. for a leaf) is turned into "sep." A flower is said to be asepalous when it has no cup or calyx. Sepal is one of the leaf-like divisions of the cup enclosing the blossom of a flower.

Ash. A.S. "Aesc." Eng. name of a group. Asec was the name given to both the tree and to a spear, but whether the tree gave its name to a spear, or the spear gave its name to the tree, each of us must settle for ourselves.

Asparagus (as-par-a-gus). G. name for the plant. Bot. name for a group.

Aspen (as-pen). A.S. "Aespen"; name for the Poplar.

Aspera (as-per-a). L. adj., rough.

Aspergilliformis (as-per-jil-li-fawm-is). L. "Aspergo" (to sprinkle); "formis" (shape); applied to little tufts which take the form of a brush. Aspergill is the name of the brush used for sprinkling Holy Water in the church.

Asperfolius (as-per-i-fo-li-us). L. "Asper" (rough); "folium" (leaf); plants with rough leaves.

Aspermous (a-sper-mus). G. "A" (no); "sperma" (seed); seedless.

Aspernata (a-sper-na-ta). L. adj., despised.

Aspersus (as-per-sus). L. adj., sprinkled.

Asperugo (as-per-u-go). L. "Asper" (rough); plants with rough leaves. Bot. name for a group.

Asperula (as-per-u-la). L. adj., roughish. Bot. name for a group.

Asperule (as-per-u-le). Eng. rendering of Asperula.

Asphodel (as-fo-del). G. name for Daffodil, sacred to

Prosperine, and considered the peculiar plant of the dead.

Aspidium (as-pi-di-um). G. "Aspidion" (a small shield); refers to the shape of the scale which shuts in the case which holds the spores. Bot. name for Shieldfern group.

Asplenium (as-ple-ni-um). G. "A" (no); "splen" (spleen). The Black Maidenhair Fern was a supposed remedy for disease of the spleen. Bot. name Spleenwort group of Ferns.

Assimilation (as-sim-il-a-shun). In plants corresponds to digestion in animals; leaves are chief organs for this.

Aster (as-ter). G. "Aster" (a star); from the look of the flower. Bot. name of a group.

Asterophyllites (as-ter-o-fil-its). G. "Aster" (a star); "phulon" (a leaf); fossil plants found in the Coal Measures having star-like whorls of leaves.

Astragal (as-tra-gal). Eng. rendering of Astragalus.

Astragalus (as-tra-gal-us). G. name for one of the bones in the heel; the root of the plant is thought to be like this bone in its shape, hence used as the bot. name of a group.

Astrantia (as-tran-shi-a). G. "Astron" (a star); from the star-like look of the flowers. Bot. name for a group.

Athamanticum (ath-a-man-ti-cum). G. After Mount Athamas, where the best quality of Meum was to be found.

Athanasia (ath-a-na-ci-a). G. "A" (not); "thanatos" (death); immortal.

Athyrium (a-thi-ri-um). G. "A" (no); "thureos"

(stone put against the door to keep it shut); refers
to the female spore-case having no lid to keep it
shut, unlike male spore-case, which has a lid. The
Ladyfern.

Atractenchyma (at-rak-teng-kim-a). G. "Atraktos"
(a spindle); "chumos" (juice); the tissue of a plant
having spindle-shaped cells.

Atratum (atra-tum). L. "Ater" (dead, black);
clothed in black.

Atriplex (a-trip-lex). G. "A" (no); "trophein"
(nourishment). Bot. name Orache group.

Atropic (a-trop-ik). G. "A" (no); "trophein"
(nourishment); plants showing degeneration of
organs.

Atropa (a-tro-pa). G. Named after Atropos, one of
the Fates, on account of the plant's deadly
poisonous properties. Bot. name for a group.

Atropous (at-ro-pus). G. "A" (no); "trope" (turning); an ovule having its original erect position.

Atrorubens (at-ro-ru-bens). L. adj., blackish red.
From "ater" (black); "rubens" (red).

Atrovirens (at-ro-vi-rens). L. adj., blackish green.
From "ater" (black); "virens" (green).

Aucuparia (aw-cu-pa-ri-a). L. "Aucupor" (bird
catching); this word is applied to the Rowan tree
in the belief that birds were made drunk from
eating the berries.

Auranticum (aw-rant-i-cum). L. adj., golden coloured;
from "arum" (gold).

Auricomus (awr-ik-om-us). L. "Auri" (of gold);
"comus" (hair); Goldilocks; the Eng. name for
one of the Buttercups.

Auricula (awr-ik-ul-a). L. "Auriculus" (a little ear);

applied from a fancied resemblance in the shape
of leaf to the ear of animals.

Auriculate (awr-ik-u-late). L. " Auriculus " (a little
ear); applied to leaves and stipules having at their
base two small ear-like lobes.

Auriculafolia (awr-ik-u-la-fol-ia). L. "Auricula " and
" folia " (a leaf); plant having its leaf like that of
the auricula.

Aurita (awr-e-ta). L. " Auris " (the ear); eared.
Second bot. name for Round Eared Willow.

Australis (aws-tra-lis). L. adj., southern.

Autophyllogeny (aw-to-fil-oj-ni). G. " Auto " (self);
" phullon " (leaf); " geneo " (producing); one leaf
growing out of another, as seen in some of the
Ferns.

Autumnalis (aw-tum-na-lis). L. adj., in the autumn.

Avellana. L. After Avella, a town of Campania
abounding in nuts, whence nuts have been called
" avellinae."

Avena (av-ena). L. name for Oats. Bot. name for
Oat group of Grasses.

Avens (av-enz). Eng. name for Guem group; is from
Welsh " afans," the name given to the Herb
Bennet.

Avenaceum (av-en-a-shum). L. adj., oat-like.

Aviculare (a-vik-u-la-re). L. " Aviculus " (a little
bird); because small birds are fond of the seeds of
this Knotweed.

Avignon-Berries. The berries of the Buckthorn
(Rhamnus). The juices of the different kinds of
Buckthorn are the raw material from which artists
and calico printers get yellow and green colours.

Avium (a-vi-um). L. "Avis" (a bird). Second bot. name of Birdcherry.

Awl-Shaped. Leaves thick at the base, tapering to a point like the shoemaker's tool, an awl, are said to be "awl-shaped."

Awl-Wort. Eng. translation of bot. name "subularia" for a group.

Awn. Swedish. "Agn" (a stiffish bristle); like that at the end of barley.

Axil (aks-il). L. "Axilla" (the armpit); the angle, on the upper side, formed by a leaf or stalk with the stem.

Axillaris (aks-il-a-ris). A bot. term, growing in the "axil."

Azalea (a-za-le-a). G. "Azo" (dry); refers to plant liking a dry soil.

B

Baccata (bak-ka-ta). L. adj., having berries from "bacca" (a berry).

Badius (bad-i-us). L. for a bay-brown colour.

Baldmoney (bawld-mun-i). Eng. name for Meum. Said to be a corruption of L. "valde bona," i.e., good money.

Ballota (ball-ot-a). G. "Ballote" (to reject); on account of the disagreeable smell of the plant. Name for one of the groups.

Balm (bam). Eng. name for Melittis.

Balsam (bawl-sam). G. "Balsamon" (name for the plant). Eng. name for Impatiens group.

Bane Berry (ban-ber-i). Eng. name for Actaea group. Gets its name bane from A.S. "bana" (murder), because of the deadly poison of the plant.

Barbarea (bar-bar-ea). After St. Barbara, to whom the
cress is dedicated. Bot. name for Watercress
group.

Barbareafolia. L. "Barbarea" (which see); "folia"
(a leaf); the plant having leaves like those of the
cress.

Barbatus (bar-bat-us). L. adj., "bearded," from
"barba" (a beard).

Barberry (bar-ber-ri). Eng. of Arabic "barbaris"
(name for the tree).

Barley (bar-li). A.S. "Bere" (barley); "lic" (like);
Eng. name for the Hordeum group.

Bartsia. After John Bartsch, a Dutch botanist, died
1738. Bot. name for a group.

Basifugal (ba-sif-u-gal). L. "Basis" (the base);
"fugeo" (to fly from); applied to the veins in
leaves which ramify from base to summit.

Basil (baz-il). G. "Basilikos," (royal); *i.e.*, the royal
herb. A highly-aromatic pot-herb, one of the
Calamints.

Basipetal (ba-sip-et-al). L. "Basis" (the base);
"peto" (to seek). The opposite of Basifugal,
veins ramify from summit to base.

Bast-Cells (bast-cells). The innermost bark next the
young wood, formed of long, tough, woody tissue.
Bast used for tying up flowers is the inner bark of
the lime tree.

Batrachion (ba-tra-ki-on). G. "Little frog." The
Butter-cup family of flowers received this as their
bot. name because they are found in ground where
little frogs abound.

Bay. Said to be a corruption of L. "bacca" (a berry).
The Bay-tree is the true Laurel of the ancients. Its

leaves were those used for the wreaths given to winners in a contest.

Beaksedge (bek-sed-ge). Eng. translation of Rhynchospora (which see). Bot. name of group of the Sedge family of Grasses.

Beam (b-em). A.S. "Beam" (a tree). Is the Eng. name for Pyrus Aria.

Bearberry (bear-ber-ri). Eng. translation of Arctostaphylos (which see). Bot. name of a group of the Heath family.

Beard Grass. Eng. translation of part (pogon) of its bot. name.

Bear's-Foot. Another name for Green Hellebore.

Becca-Bunga (bek-a-bun-ja). Flemish. "Mouthsmart"; because of the pungency of the leaf. Second bot. name for Brooklime.

Bedegar (bed-e-gar). Persian name for a spongy excrescence found on rose bushes, caused by the puncture of a small insect.

Bed-Straw. Eng. name for Galium verum. Said to have been the straw in the manger where the Saviour was born. The common expression "being in straw," as applied to women when confined, is said to be due to the use of the plant as their bedding. So "they" say.

Beech. A.S. "Bece" (the name for the tree). Our word "book."

Begonia (be-go-ni-a). Named after Begon, a French botanist.

Belladonna (bel-la-don-na). Italian. "Bella" (pretty); "donna" (lady); refers to the use of the plant by ladies for enlarging the pupil of the eye and generally brightening it up. Second bot. name for Deadly Nightshade.

Bellis (bel-lis). L. adj., "pretty." Bot. name for Daisy group.

Bellidifolia (bel-id-i-fol-ia). L. "Bellis" (a daisy); "folia" (leaves); having leaves like those of the Daisy.

Bennet (ben-et). L. adj., "benedictus" (praised). The second half of the name—Herb-bennet—is apparently a corruption of the L. adj. Another name for Common Avens.

Bents. Is the common name for dry stalks of withered grass.

Berberideæ (ber-ber-i-de). L. "berberis" and G. "oides" (like). Bot. name for Barberry family (Berberis).

Berberis (ber-ber-is). L. name for some tree or shrub; derived from Arabic "berberi" (wild). Bot. name Barberry group.

Bermuda-Grass. Another name for Creeping Cyndon.

Berry. Is a fruit having a skin which contains pulpy or fleshy juice in which there are a number of seeds. The word itself is said to be a corruption of the Keltic word "bier" (produce).

Beta (be-ta). L. name for Beetroot. Said to be so called because the seed is like the shape of the Greek letter "b." Or from the Keltic "bett" (red), from the colour of the root. Bot. name for Beet group.

Betel (bet-l). The leaves of a pepper plant much chewed with areca-nut and lime by the natives of India.

Betonica (be-ton-ik-a). Derived by changing the "v."

into "b" from vetonica, as the plant was called in Gaul. Second bot. name of Betony.

Betony (bet-o-ni). A corruption of second L. bot. name.

Betula (bet-u-la). L. name of Birch tree. Bot. name Birch group.

Betulus (bet-u-lus). Second bot. name Common Hornbeam.

Bi. A common L. prefix meaning two.

Bibracteata (bi-brak-te-a-ta). L. "Bi" (two); "bractea" (thin metal leaves). The modified leaves at the base of the flowerstalk are called "bracts," when very small "scales."

Bicapsular (bi-kap-su-ler). L. "Bi" (two); "capsula" (a little chest); i.e., having two pods or seed vessels.

Bicarinate (bi-kar-in-at). L. "Bi" (two); "carina" (keels); two-keeled.

Bicarpel (bi-kar-pel). L. "Bi" (two), "carpel" (carpel); i.e., when the pistil is divided into two separate and distinct female organs.

Bicolor (bi-kol-or). L. "Bi" (two); "color" (colours); variegated.

Bidens (bi-dens). L. "Bi" (two); "dens" (teeth); refers to the two tooth-like projections on the fruit of Bur-Marigold. Bot. name for a group.

Bidentate (bi-den-tat). L. "Bi" (two); "dens" (teeth); when the teeth along the margin of a leaf are also in turn toothed.

Biennials (bi-en-ni-als). L. "Bi" (two); "annus" (a year); applied to plants that do not bear flowers till the second year and then die down.

Bifid (bi-fid). L. "Bi" (two); "fidi" (cleft); cleft in two, but not deeply divided.

Bifoliate (bi-fo-li-at). L. " Bi " (two); "folia " (leaves); the leaf having two leaflets.

Bifolia (bi-fo-li-a). L. adj., " two-leaved."

Biglumis (bi-glu-mis). L. " Bi " (two); " glumis " (husk); the outer covering that protects the flowers of Grasses and Rushes.

Bijugate (bi-joo-gat). L. " Bi ". (two); " jugum " (a yoke); having two pairs of leaflets.

Bilabiate (bi-la-bi-at). L. " Bi " (two); " labium " (a lip); having two lips.

Bilamellar (bi-lam-el-lar). L. "Bi" (two); " lamina " (plates); having two plates.

Bilberry (bil-ber-ri). A.S. " Blea " (blue); refers to dark blue colour of the fruit.

Bilobate (bi-lo-bat). L. " bi " (two); G. " lobos " (lobe of the ear); *i.e.,* two-lobed.

Bilocular (bi-lok-u-ler). L. " Bi " (two); " loculus " (a little place); *i.e.,* two-celled.

Binate (bi-nat). L. " Binnus "; two and two; a binate leaf has a simple stalk connecting two leaflets at the top.

Bindweed. Eng. name for Convolvulus group.

Binervate (bi-ner-vat). L. " Bi " (two); " nervus " (nerve); two-nerved. A nerve is the larger vein found on leaves.

Biogenesis (bi-o-jen-e-sis). G. "Bios" (life); "genesis" (origin); the production of living cells from similar cells; sexual generation.

Biophagus (bi-of-a-gus). G. "Bios" (life); "phago" (eat); applied to plants that catch and eat insects.

Bipetalous (bi-pet-a-lus). L. " bi " (two); G. " petalon " (a leaf); two-petalled.

Bipinnate (bi-pin-nat). L. " Bi " (two); " pinna " (a

BOTANICAL NAMES

feather; having pinnate (which see) leaves on both sides of leaf-stalk.

Bipinnatified (bi-pin-nat-i-fid). L. "Bi" (two); "pinna" (feather); "fidi" (cleft); when the pinnate leaflets are again each pinnated.

Biramus (bi-ra-mus). L. "Bi" (two); "ramus" (a branch); a limb divided into two branches.

Birch. Eng. name for Betula group; Birch, from A.S. "beorc," the bark-tree.

Birdcherry. Eng. name for one of the three wild Cherries, and gets the name "bird" because the fruit is only fit for birds.

Bird's Foot. Eng. translation of the bot. name Ornithopus, a group of the Pea family. The seed vessels of the plant are like the claw of a bird.

Bird's Nest. Eng. name for Neottia group, and is a translation of the L. second name of the only plant in that group. It is said to have got this name because the roots of the plant are entangled like the sticks in a crow's nest.

Birostrate (bi-ros-trat). L. "Bi" (two); "rotrum" (a beak); double beaked.

Bishop's-Weed. A name used in the 16th century for what is now known as Gout-weed.

Biserrate (bi-ser-rat). L. "Bi" (twice); "serra" (a saw); some leaves are notched round their margin with saw-like teeth, and these in turn are notched in the same way.

Bistorta (bis-tort-a). L. "Bis" (twice); "totus" (twisted); refers to the twisted appearance of the root.

Biternate (bi-ter-nat). L. "Bi" (twice); "terni"

(three & three); leaves divided into three leaflets, each of these divided into three in their turn.

Bithynica (bi-thin-i-ka). After Bithynia, an ancient name of one of the divisions of Asia Minor.

Bitter Cress. Eng. name for Cardimine group.

Bittersweet. Eng. translation of "Dulcamara," the second bot. name for Nightshade.

Bivalve (bi-valv). L. "Bi" (two); "valva" (leaf of a folding-door); a seed vessel which consists of two parts joined by a hinge.

Black Bryony. Eng. name for Tamus group.

Bladder Fern. Eng. name for, and translation of, "Cystopteris." The bot. name of a group.

Bladder Wort. Eng. name for, and translation of, "Utricularia." The bot. name of a group.

Blade. Botanically is the green part of the leaf alone without its stalk.

Blaeberry. Scotch for "Bilberry" (which see).

Blastocolla (blas-to-kol-la). G. "Blastos" (a bud); "kolla" (glue); the gummy substance often found on young buds.

Blattaria (blat-ter-ia). L. "Blatta" (a moth); because the leaves, being sticky, catch moths. Second bot. name for Moth Mullein.

Blechnum (blek-num). G. "Blechnon," (a fern). Bot. name for Blechnum group.

Blennius (blen-ni-us). G. "Blenna" (slime); refers to the characteristic of some part.

Bletting (blet-ting). L. "Bliteus" (tasteless); the change that occurs in the pulp of fruit after being kept for some time.

Blinks. A common name for Chick Weed.

Blite (blit). L. "Blitum" was the old name for Wild

Amaranth, but by changing the "um" into "e,"
an Eng. word is formed, and now given to Sea-
Blite.

Blysmus (blis-mus). G. "Blusmos" (a spring), because the plant loves wet places. Bot. name for
a group.

Bocconi (bok-ko-ni). After Bocconi. Second bot.
name for Boccone's Clover.

Boehmeri (boeh-mer-i). After Boehmer. Second bot.
name for the Grass "Boehmer's Phleum."

Bog Orchis. Eng. name for Malaxis group.

Bonus-Henricus (bo-nus hen-ri-cus). L. for "Good
Henry"; so called to distinguish it from a
poisonous plant called "Bad Henry." Grim says
that Henry here is not a Christian name, but has
reference to Elves and Kobolds, in German called
Heinz and Heinrich. Someone has made the Eng.
name more puzzling by calling this plant—a Goosefoot—Good "King" Henry.

Borage (bor-aj). Eng. name for the group Borago.
In former days Borage was noted as one of the
four "cordial flowers," most worthy of esteem for
cheering the spirit, Rose, Violet and Alkanet being
the other three.

Boragineæ (bor-aj-in-e-ae). From "Borago." Bot.
name for the Borage family.

Borago (bor-a-go). L. "Borra" (a rough hair); from
a characteristic of the plant. Is the bot. name for
Borage group.

Borealis (bor-e-a-lis). L. adj., "northern"; from
Boreas, the North Wind.

Borkhausia (bork-haus-i-a). Named after Borkhausen,
a German botanist, died 1806.

Boronia (bo-ro-ni-a). After Borone, an Italian botanist.

Bothrenchyma (both-reng-kim-a). G. "Bothros" (a pit); "engchuma" (anything poured in); pitted vessels with depressions inside their walls.

Bothrodendron (both-ro-den-dron). G. "Bothros" (a pit); "dendron" (a tree); fossil trees of Club-moss, found in the Coal Measures having stems with a pitted surface.

Botany. G. "Botane" (a plant).

Botrychium (bot-rik-i-um). G. "Botrus" (a bunch of grapes); from the appearance of the fertile fronds. Is the bot. name for Moon Wort group of Ferns.

Botrys (bot-ris). G. "Botrus" (a bunch of grapes). Second bot. name Cut-leaved Germander.

Bourgeon (ber-jon). French for the young shoots of the vine. Trees are said to be "burgeoning" when, in the early spring, the buds begin to break forth.

Box. Eng. name for Buxus group. The Eng. word is but a contraction of the L. word Buxus.

Brachiate (bra-ki-at). G. "Brachion" (an arm); having the opposite pairs of branches placed at right angles to each other.

Brachy (brak-i). G. "Brachus" (short); a prefix often used in scientific words.

Brachycarpum (brak-i-kar-pum). G. "Brachy" (short); "carpus" (fruit); short carpels (which see).

Brachypodium (brak-i-pod-i-um). G. "Brachy" (short); "podium" (a little foot); refers to the Spikelet or Grassflower being short. Bot. name for False Brome group.

Brachystemon (brak-i-stem-on). G. "Brachy" (short); "stemon" (stamen); i.e., short stamens.

Bracken (brak-en). Swedish. "Bracken" (a fern); our most common fern.

Bracts (brakts). L. "Bractea" (a thin leaf of metal); are small modified leaves or scales from the centre of which the flower bud grows.

Bracteate (brak-te-at). Having bracts.

Bracteole (brak-te-ol).

Bractlet (brackt-let). A small bract at the base of the flower stalk.

Braird (brard). A.S. "Brord" (a point); the first leaves of corn that show themselves.

Brake. Another name for Bracken.

Bramble. A.S. "Brembel" (a thorny bush).

Brank. Is the Gaelic for Buckwheat (which see).

Brassica (bras-i-ka. L. "Brassica" (a cabbage). Bot. name for a group to which many culinary plants belong.

Brevisetum (brev-i-se-tum). L. "Brvis" (small); from a characteristic feature.

Brevipes (brev-i-pes). L. "Brevis" (short); "pes" (foot or stalk); short stalked.

Bristle Fern (bris-sel-fern). A.S. "Bristel"; when the hairs of the plant are stiff and round. Eng. name for Trichomanes group.

Briza (bri-sa). G. "Brizo" (to hang the head as in sleep). Bot. name for Quakergrass group.

Broccoli (brok-ko-li). Italian. "Broccoli" (sprouts); a variety of the Cauliflower.

Brome (brom). Eng. name for Bromus group.

Bromus (bro-mus). G. name for Oates. Bot. name for Brome group.

Brooklime. Is said to mean brook-mud. It is the

Broklempke of old writers, but now used as Eng. name of one of the Speedwells.

Bromoides (bro-moi-des). G. "Bromus" and "oides" (like); Brome-like.

Broom. A.S. "Brom" (name of plant). Name for Cytisus group.

Broomrape. Eng. name for Orobranche group and also family. The plants of the group are parasites, growing on the Broom and Furze roots; the base of the plant is swollen somewhat turnip-like, and as "rape" was Eng. rendering of L. "rapum" (a turnip), it looks as if Broomrape is Broomturnip.

Brumalis (bro-mal-is). L. adj., "wintery"; from "bruma" (winter).

Brunella (bra-nel-la). See Prunella.

Bruscus (brus-cus). See Ruscus.

Bryology (bri-ol-o-ji). G. "Bruon" (moss); "logos" (discourse); the study of Mosses.

Bryonia (bri-o-nia). G. "Bruo" (to abound). Bot. name Bryony group.

Bryony (bri-o-ni). Eng. name for Bryonia group. There are two Bryonys—the Common Bryony belongs to the Bryony group; the Black Bryony to the Tamus group.

Buckbean. Name of doubtful origin. Some say it is corrupted Dutch for "bocks-boonen," which in its turn is a corruption of L. "scorbutus" (scurvy); others, that "buck" is corrupted "bog." Bot. name Menyanthes group.

Buck's Horn. Eng. name for the only Plantain that has a divided leaf.

Buckthorn. "Buck" (a corruption of "box"). Bot.

name Rhamnus group; the plants of this group
yield sap-green and a yellow dye.

Buckwheat. Danish. " Bock-weit " (beech wheat);
because the seeds are like those of the beech.
Sometimes grown as food for pheasants. See
Fagopyrum.

Bud. Small protruberance, covered with scales, on
stem or branch, which contain future flower or leaf;
popularly called " eyes."

Bufonius (bu-fon-i-us). L. " Bufo " (a toad). Second
bot. name Toad-rush.

Bugle (bu-gl). Eng. corruption of L. name " abuja."
Eng. name for Ajuga group.

Bugloss (bu-glos). G. " Bous " (an ox); " gloss " (a
tongue); because of the shape and roughness of the
leaf. Eng. name Lycopis group. Used in the
Eng. name—Viper's Bugloss—for one of the
Echium group.

Bulb. L. " Bulbus " (a globular root); a round mass
of fleshy scales, from which the roots grow down-
wards, the stem upwards.

Bulbil (bulb-il).

Bulblet (bulb-let). " Axillary " (see Axillaris) bulbs
produced by some of the lilies.

Bulbiferous (bulb-if-er-ous). L. adj. " producing bulbs ";
from " bulbus " (a globular root); " ferous "
(bearing).

Bulbosus (bul-bo-sus). L. adj., " containing bulbs."

Bulbocastanum (bul-bo-cas-tan-um). L. " Bulbus "
(a globular root); " castanea " (a chestnut).
Second bot. name for one of the Carum group.
Refers to the tubers found on the roots known as
Pig-nuts or Earth-nuts.

Bullace (bool-las). Irish. "Bulos" (a prune); the Wild Plum, a variety of the Sloe.

Bullate (bool-at). L. "Bulla" (a bubble); when the skin of the leaf rise up in blisters.

Bullrush. Common name for reed plants growing in pools; they were formerly called "Pool-rush," now corrupted to Bullrush.

Bunium (bun-i-um). G. "Bounos" (a hill); refers to the plant growing on the hills rather than in the valley. A synonym for first Bot. name—Tuberous Carum (the Earth-nut).

Bunt. A fungoid disease which attacks Wheat. (See Smut.)

Buplever (bu-plev-er). Eng. rendering of Bupleurum.

Bupleurum (bu-plo-rum). G. "Buos" (an ox); "pleuron" (a rib); from the ribbed leaves of the plant. Bot. name Buplever group. The Thorough-Wax of old Herbalists.

Bur. Gaelic. "Bior" (a small thorn); is the rough prickly envelope enclosing the seeds of many plants.

Bur-dock. "Bur" and "dock"; the dock of many burs. Eng. name for Arctium group.

Burgamot. From the French; a variety of the pear.

Burging. See Bougeon.

Burlace. A corruption of "burdelais" (a kind of grape).

Burnet (ber-net). A corruption of "Brunette"; refers to the colour of the flower.

Burrel. A variety of pear; also called Red-Butter-Pear.

Bur-Weed. Eng. name for Xanthium group.

Bursicule (burs-i-kul). L. A little purse, from "bursa" (a purse). Is the shape the upper part of the stigma of an orchid sometimes takes.

Bursa-Pastores (bur-sa-pas-tor-is). A rendering in Latin of the common name "Shepherd's Purse"; the shape of the seed pods being like the old-fashioned bag-purse; from the L. "bursa" (a purse); "pastoris" (of a shepherd).

Bush. Is a low shrub, much branched from near the roots.

Butcher's Broom. Is the common name for Ruscus; is also called Knee Holly. Said to be called Butcher's Broom because the butchers used it to sweep their blocks. Sometimes known as Jews' Myrtle, because it is sold for use during the Feast of Tabernacles.

Butome. Eng. rendering of Butomus.

Butomus (bu-to-mus). G. "Bou" (an ox); "tenno" (to cut); because the sharp edge of the leaf cuts the mouth of cattle. Bot. name for Butome group.

Butter Bur. Common name for one of the Colt's Foots.

Butter Cup. The common name for several Ranunculus, and given because of the bright yellow, and shape of the flowers.

Butter Wort. Common name for Pengicula group, insectivorous, marsh plants. Gets the name butter from the greasy feel of the leaves. To make a kind of cream cheese, Laplanders put the leaves into the reindeer milk. The leaves do not act in the same way in cow's milk.

Buxus (buks-us). G. "Pyxos" (name for the Box). Bot. name for Box group.

Buxhaumii (buks-hau-mi. After Buxhaum, a botanist, who lived about 1727.

Byssus (bis-sus). L. name for Flax; is the silky tufts of mould growing on damp decaying substances.

C

Cabbage. French, through L. "caboche" (round-headed); the well-known vegetable.

Caber (ka-ber). Gaelic: "Caber" (the trunk of a tree); is the pole used in one of the Highland games.

Cactus (kak-tus). L. name for some sort of prickly plant; now applied to a large family of plants having fleshy, prickly leaf and stem.

Caducous (ka-du-kus). L. adj., "falling early"; a tendency for leaf or petal to fall off early.

Cærulium (se-ru-li-um). L. "Caerulus" (sky-blue); blue.

Cæsius (se-zhi-us). L. adj., "grey"; bluish-grey.

Cæspitosa (ses-pi-toza). L. "Caespitem" (a knot or tuft); applied to plants which grow in tufts.

Cakile (ka-kil). Name for Sea-Rocket. The word is an old Arabic name for this or some similar plant. Bot. name for one of the groups.

Caladium (ka-la-di-um). G. "Kalos" (beautiful); name of some variegated foliage plants.

Calamagrostis (kal-am-ag-ros-tis). G. "Kalam" (a reed); "agrostis" (of the field). Bot. name for Small-Reed group.

Calamint (ka-la-mint). Eng. for Calamintha.

Calamintha (kal-a-min-tha). G. "Kala" (good); "mintha" (mint). Bot. name for Calamint group.

Calamites (kal-am-i-tes). L. "Calamus" (a red); name given to some fossil stems found in the Coal Measures, and so called because they resemble gigantic reeds.

Calamus (kal-a-mus). L. "Calamus" (a reed). Second bot. name Sweet Sedge.

Calcarea (kal-kar-ea). L. "Calcar" (a spur); when the petal or petals form into a spur.

Calcareum (kal-kar-eum). L. adj., from "calx" (lime). A second bot. name applied to plant that grows on limestone.

Calceolaria (kal-si-o-la-ri-a). L. "Calceolus" (a little shoe"); from the shoe-like shape of the flower.

Calceolus (kal-si-o-lus). See above. Second bot. name for Lady's Slipper.

Calcitrapa (kal-cit-ra-pa). L. "Caltrops" (name given to iron balls covered with spikes, used to lame cavalry horses). Second bot. name for Star Thistle from its spikes.

Calenduliflorum (ka-len-du-li-flo-rum). L. "Calendæ" (the first day of a month); a term applied to certain flowers, including the Marigold, because a specimen can be found in every month of the year.

Callitriche (kal-li-trik-e). G. "Kali" (beautiful); "trichos" (hair); from the slender hair-like stems. Bot. name for a group.

Callitrichoneæ (kal-li-trik-en-e). See above. Bot. name for a family.

Calluna (kal-lu-na). G. "Kalluno" (to cleanse with a broom made of heather). Bot. name for Ling group.

Caltha (kal-tha). G. "Kalthos" (a cup). Bot. name for Caltha group.

Calvatus (kal-va-tus). L. "Calva" (bald); i.e., naked.

Calycinum (kal-e-sin-um). G. "Kalux" (a covering husk or shell). Second bot. of some plants.

Calycanthus (kal-e-kan-thus). G. "Calyx" (a flower-cup); "anthus" (a flower); applied when the green leaves (sepals) are coloured like the petals of the flower.

Calystigia (kal-e-stig-ia). G. "Kalos" (beautiful); "stege" (covering); two of the Bindweeds are distinguished by this name, because of the large size of their bracts.

Calyx (ka-liks). G. "Kalux" (a husk or covering); is a protection to the flower when in bud, and forms a cup for it when it opens out; the separate leaves which make up the cup are—botanically—called sepals.

Cambrica (kam-bri-ka). From Cambrica, the ancient name for Wales. Is the second bot. name for the Welsh Poppy.

Camelina (ka-mel-e-na). G. "Chamai" (on the ground); "linon" (flax). Bot. name for a group.

Campanula (kam-pan-u-la). L. "Campanula" (a little bell); from the shape of the flower. Bot. name for a group.

Campanulaceæ (kam-pan-u-la-si-a). L. "Campanula" and "aceus" (like). Bot. name for a family.

Campestris (kam-pes-tris). L. "Campus" (afield, *i.e.*, belonging to the field). A common second bot. name applied to many plants.

Campion (kam-pi-on). Unknown. Hulme suggests it may be from "campus" (a field), since these flowers are often found there.

Canadensis (ka-na-den-sis). L. for "of Canada," whence it was introduced into England in 1847. Is the second bot. name for the Water-Thyme; also known as the American Waterweed.

Canariensis (kan-ar-i-en-sis). L. "Belonging to the canary." Second bot. name of the grass—Phalaris —the seed of which is known as Canary seed.

Canary Grass. Eng. name for Phalaris canariensis.

Candicus (kan-di-cus).

Candidus (kan-did-us). L. "Candeo" (to shine); *i.e.*, whitish colour.

Candytuft. "Candy," from Candia in Crete; "tuft," from its bunch or tuft of flowers, is the Eng. name for Iberis group.

Canescens (ka-nes-sens). L. "Canus" (grey); *i.e.*, of a greyish colour.

Canina (ka-nina).

Caninum (ka-ninum). L. "Belonging to a dog," *i.e.*, something common; we say dog-rose, dog-violet, &c.

Cannabis (kan-na-bis). G. name for Hemp.

Canterbury Bells. These flowers were so named by Gerarde from their growing plentifully in the low woods about Canterbury.

Caper (ka-per). The flower-bud of the caper-bush.

Capillaris (kap-il-lar-is). L. "Capillus" (hair); *i.e.*, hair-like.

Capillus-Veneris (kap-il-lus-Ven-er-is). L. "Capillus" (hair); "Veneris" (of Venus). Second bot. name Maiden-Hair Fern.

Capitatus (kap-e-ta-tus). L. "Caput" (a head). Second bot. name Capitate Rush, because the flowers grow in clusters as in the Composite family.

Caprea (kap-rea). L. "Caper" (a goat). Second bot. name for Sallow, one of the Willows. Goats are fond of Willow Catkins.

5

Caprifolium (kap-re-fol-ium). L. " Caper " (a goat);
   " folium " (a leaf). Second bot. name Perfoliate
   Honeysuckle.

Caprifoliaceæ (kap-re-fol-i-acea). (See above, with
   " aceus " (like) added.) Bot. name for Honeysuckle family.

Capreolate (kap-re-o-late). L. " Capreolus " (a
   tendril); having tendrils.

Capsell. Eng. rendering of Capsella.

Capsella (kap-sel-la). L. " Capsella " (a little box);
   from the shape of seed vessel. Bot. name of a
   group.

Capsicum (kap-se-cum). L. " Capsa " (a box); from
   the shape of the pod. Cayenne Pepper gets its
   name from having first come from that country, and
   is the dried powdered fruit of the plant.

Capsule (kap-sewl). L. " Capsula " (a little chest).
   Is the bot. name for the seed-vessel of plants, commonly known as pods or pouches. When the fruit
   is ripe, the capsule dry up, split open, scattering
   their seed.

Caraway (kar-a-wa). Arabic. " Karwiya," the name
   for Caraway Seeds.

Cardamine (kard-a-mine). G. " Cardia " (the heart);
   " damao " (to strengthen); from the properties of
   the plant on the heart. Bot. name for a group.

Cardiaca (kar-de-aka). G. " Cardia " (the heart);
   from the effects on the heart; more especially in
   the case of pregnant women. See Motherwort, for
   which this is second bot. name.

Cardoon (kar-doon). Directly from French " char-
   don "; indirectly from L. " carduus " (a thistle); a

garden vegetable of Artichoke family, used in salads.

Carduus (kar-du-us). L. name for thistle. Bot. name. Thistle group.

Carex (ka-rex). L. name for some kind of Sedge. Now used as the bot. name for one of the groups of that family.

Caricis (ka-ri-sis).

Caricina (ka-ri-sina). Both L. "Carex" (sedge); *i.e.*, sedge-like.

Carinata (kar-e-nata). L. "Carina" (the keel of a ship). Second bot. name for Keeled Cornsalad.

Carlina (kar-le-na). L. "Carolus" (Charles); named after Charlemagne, because the root of the plant had been given to him by an angel as a cure for the plague which decimated his army. Bot. name Carline group.

Carline (kar-line). See above.

Carnation (kar-na-shun). Derivation disputed : (1) "carnis" (flesh), because the colour of the flower is flesh coloured; (2) a corruption of "coronation," the flower being used for chaplets.

Carnea (kar-ne-a). L. adj., "fleshy." Second bot. name Mediterranean Heath. From its colour.

Carolinianum (kar-o-lin-i-anum). Second bot. name American variety Cut-leaved Geranium.

Carolorum (kar-o-lo-rum). See Carlina. This is a more Latinized form of that.

Carota (kar-o-ta). L. form of the word "carrot," supposed to be derived from the Keltic "car," meaning red, from the colour of the root of the plant.

Carpel (kar-pel). G. "Karpos" (fruit); a seed-vessel,

being a modified leaf forming the pistil of the flower.

Carpinus (kar-pi-nus). From the Keltic " car " (wood); " pinus " (a head); because from the wood of the tree the yokes for oxen were made, hence its Eng. name, Hornbeam. Bot. name for Hornbeam group.

Carpinifolius (kar-pin-i-fo-li-us). " Carpinus " (see above); " folius " (a leaf); *i.e.*, Hornbeamed-leaved.

Carrot (kar-rut). See Carota.

Carum (kar-um). L. name for Caraway, derived through the G. from the name of the country Caria, where it grew abundantly.

Carui (kar-u-i).

Carvi (kar-vi). L. Other forms of " carum," which see.

Caryophyllaceæ (kar-e-o-fil-a-seus). G. " Karuon " (a nut); " phullon " (a leaf); *i.e.*, the " nut-leaved " Indian plant, now known as Clove-tree; with the L. suffix " aceus " (like) added. Is the bot. name for Pink family.

Caryophyllea (kar-e-o-fil-lea. See above. Second bot. name for one of the Aira group of Grasses.

Caspia (kas-pi-a). After the Caspian Sea. Second bot. name Matted Sea Lavendar. Found in the salt marshes of Norfolk only.

Castaneus (kas-ta-neus. L. " Castanea " (a chestnut); *i.e.*, chestnut coloured. Castana, a town of Thessaly, was renowned for its chestnut trees.

Catabrosa (kat-a-bro-sa). G. " Catabrosis " (gnawed). This is the bot. name for a group, having only one species; so named from the gnawed-like look of its

"glumes," as the outer covering of the flowers of
grasses are botanically called.

Catalpa (ka-tal-pa). Said to be a corruption of
Catawba, the name of river in North Carolina,
U.S., on the banks of which Catesby found these
trees.

Catapodium (kat-a-po-di-um). G. "Kata" (below);
"podos" (the foot); name for a new division in
which some of the grasses are included.

Cataria (ka-tar-ia). L. "Catus" (a male cat). Second
bot. name for Catmint, because cats are supposed
to like the smell of the plant.

Catharticus (ka-thar-ti-kus). G. word for a purgative.
Second bot. name applied to one of the Flax, because of the medicinal properties of the plant.

Catkin (kat-kin). Dutch "kattekin" (a little cat); are
the blossoms of the willow, and so called because
of their resemblance to a cat's tail.

Caucalis (kau-kal-is). G. name for some umbelliferous
herb. Now used as the bot. name of a group.

Cauliflower. G. "caulos" (a stalk); Eng. "flower";
i.e., the flower of many stalks.

Cavatifolius (kav-at-i-fol-i-us). L. "Cavus" (hollow);
"folius" (leaf); applied to some one of the
varieties of the Bramble.

Cayenne (kay-en). The capital of French Guiana. See
Capsicum.

Cedar (se-dar). G. name for the tree. Is a group of
the cone-bearing family.

Celandine (sel-an-dine). A corruption of G. "chelidon" (a swallow); and said to have been given as
a name to the plants because they come into
blossom when the swallow arrive. There are two

Celandines—one belongs to the Poppy group, the other to the Buttercup group.

Celastraceæ (sel-as-tra-se-a). Bot. name for Celastrus family. The Spindle tree (which see) is the only one of the family we have.

Celery (seler-e). Or Sellery. Is a corruption of G. "selinon" (parsley). Grows wild by the sea; in its wild state it is poisonous, but when earthed up, thus preventing the leaves being acted upon by light, the poisonous properties do not develop.

Celerata (sel-er-a-ta). L. adj., "quick," from L. "celer."

Centaurea (sen-taw-rea). G. "Centaur" (a fabulous being, half-man, half-horse). Bot. name for a group. One of the Centaurs, Chiron, was accidentally wounded by an arrow poisoned with the blood of the Hydrea. Being learned in the medicinal properties of herbs, by means of the Blue-bottle or Cornflower, one of this group, he healed the wound. Jupiter placed him among the constellations, where he is called Sagittarius the Archer.

Centaury (sen-taw-re). Is the Eng. name for a group, and is a translation of the second bot. name Centaurium. See Centaurea.

Centranth (sen-tranth). Eng. rendering of Centranthus.

Centranthus (sen-tranth-us). G. "Centron" (a spur); "anthos" (a flower). Bot. name for a group of Valerian family, because the Red Valerian has a distinct spur.

Centuncule. Eng. for Centunculus.

Centunculus (sen-tun-cu-lus). L. "Cento" (patchwork); *i.e.*, "a little patch." Bot. name for a group.

Cephalanthera (sef-al-an-thera). G. "Cephale" (a head); "anthos" (a flower). Bot. name for a group of Orchid family.

Cerast (ser-ast). Eng. name for Cerastium.

Cerastium (ser-ast-i-um). G. "Ceras" (a horn); from the horn-like shape of some of the seed pods. Bot. name for a group.

Cerasus (ser-a-sus). G. "Kerasos," as the Cherry tree was called, having been introduced from Cerasus in Pontus.

Cerastoides. G. "Ceras" and "oides" (like); *i.e.*, in some respect resembling the Cherry tree.

Ceratophyllum (ser-at-o-fil-lum). G. "Cerat" (a horn); "phyllom" (a leaf); from the horn-like look of the forked leaves. Bot. name for Hornwort group.

Cerefolium (se-re-fol-i-um). A Latinized form of Chaerophyllum, an old name for Chervil (which see).

Cerinthoides (se-rin-tho-i-des). G. "Kerinthos" (bee-bread; "oides" (like). Second bot. name for Honeywort Hawkweed.

Cernus (ser-nus). L. adj., "with face hanging down-wards looking to earth." Applied as second bot. name to Bur-Marigold.

Ceterach (set-er-ak). The Arabic name of some plant now used as bot. name for a group of the Fern family.

Chaerophyllum (ker-o-fil-lum). G. "Chairo" (to re-joice); "phyllon" (a leaf); from the sweet smell of the leaf. Bot. name for the Chervil group.

Chamaedrys (kam-a-drys). G. "Chamae" (on the ground); "drys" (an oak). This is the name that a Greek physician, Dioscorides, who lived in the beginning of the Christian era, and wrote of plants, gave to the plants now known as Germander. Second bot. name for Wall Germander.

Chamaemorus (kam-a-mor-us). G. "Chamae" (ground); "morus" (mulberry). Second bot. name for Cloudberry.

Chamaepitys (kam-a-pit-is). G. "Chamae" (ground); "pitys" (pine). Second bot. name for Yellow Bugle; also called Ground Pine.

Chamaegrostis (kam-ag-ros-tis). G. "Chamae" (ground); "agrostis" (the country); a synonym for 1st bot. name Mibora group.

Chamomilla (kam-o-mil-la). G. "Chamo" (earth); "melon," (an apple); from the smell of the flower being like that of an apple. Second bot. name for Wild Chamomile.

Chamomile (kam-a-mil). See above. Eng. name for Anthemis group.

Chara (ka-ra).

Characeæ (ka-ra-se-a). Or Stonewort. Are a small group of water plants growing at the bottom of ponds or shallow lakes. It looks as if they are a degenerate offspring of gigantic ancestors, who helped to make the coal we now burn. A most interesting family on account of its peculiar characteristic method of reproduction.

Charlock (char-lok). A modern rendering of A.S. "cerlice" (wild mustard). Bot. name Brassica Sinapis.

Cheiri (ki-ri).

Cheiranthus (ki-ran-thus). G. "Cheiri" is the second
bot. name for the Wallflower. Cheiranthus, *i.e.*,
"Cheiri," "flower," is the bot. name for the Wallflower group. Alcock, in his "Botanic Names for
English Readers," says that "Kheyry" was the
Arabic name of a red-coloured sweet-scented flower.
The Greeks gave this name to the Wallflower. Per-
chance it had been introduced from Arabia. Any-
how, "cheiri" in Greek means a "hand." So
some one hunting for the meaning of the G. name
said it was "Handflower," and so called because,
being sweet-smelling, it was carried in the hand.
This illustrates how difficult it is to find out how
and why flowers came by their name. (See Wallflower on this point.)

Cheiranthoides (ki-ran-thoi-des). G. "Chreianthus"
and "oides" (like); *i.e.*, wallflower-like. Second
bot. name Treacle Mustard.

Chelidonium (ke-li-do-ni-um). G. "Chelidon" (a
swallow. (See Celandine.) Bot. name for a group.

Chenopodiaceæ (ken-o-po-di-ase-e). G. "Chenopodium." and "aceus" (like). Bot. name for the
Goosefoot family.

Chenopodium (ken-o-po-di-um). G. "Chen" (a
goose); "pous" (a foot); from the shape of the
leaf. Bot. name for a group Goosefoot family.
Some of the plants of this family were, in days of
old, much used as a vegetable, now replaced by
Spinach.

Cherleri (cher-ler-i). Named after Cherler, the botanist,
who died 1610. Second bot. name Cyphel, Sand-
wort group.

Cherry. See Cerasus.

Chervil (cher-vil). From A.S. " cerfille,"—which in turn was a corruption of " Cerefolium " (which see).

Chickweed. So called because the plant is given to caged birds. Its seeds, found throughout the year, furnish food for many little birds.

Chicory (chik-or-e). Popular name for Chicorium (which see).

Chives. From the French " cive " (a small onion without a bulb). Is the Eng. name for one of Allium group Lily family.

Chlora (klo-ra). G. " Chloros " (yellowish green); from the colour of the flowers. Bot. name for a group.

Chlorantha (klo-ran-tha). G. " Chloros " (yellowish green); " anthus " (a flower). Second bot. name of a variety of the Butterfly Orchid, but the colour of its flower is usually pure white, not "yellowish green," as its botanical name would lead one to think.

Cloodes (klo-o-des). G. " ckloodes " (grass green). Second bot. name variety Common Centaury.

Chlorophyll (klo-ro-fil). G. " Chloros " (green); " phyllon " (a leaf); the green colouring matter of plants.

Christopher (kris-to-fer). Herb Christopher was a common name at one time for the Bane-berry. Christopher was a saint of the Roman Catholic and Greek Churches, who suffered martyrdom under the Emperor Decius 249-251.

Chromule (kro-mul). G. " Chroma " (a colour); the colouring matter of plants other than green.

Chrysanthemum (kry-san-the-mum). G. " Chrys "

(golden); "anthus" (a flower); *i.e.,* golden-
flowered). Bot. name for a group.

Chryscoma (kris-co-ma). G. "Chrys" (golden);
"coma" (locks); *i.e.,* Goldilocks.

Chrysosplene (kris-o-splen-e). Eng. for Chrisosplenium.

Chrysosplenium (kris-o-splen-i-um). G. "Chrys"
(golden); "splenium" (the spleen). The Golden
Saxifrage was supposed to be a golden physic for
the spleen. Bot. name for the group of the Saxifrage family.

Cicely (sis-e-li). A corruption of G. "sessele" (the
name for the plant. Eng. name for Myrrhis group.

Cicendia (si-send-ia). G. "Kikinnos" (curled hair);
from the entangled, slender stems and branches.
Bot. name for a group.

Cichorium (chi-kor-i-um). A Latinized form of the
Arabic "chikouryeh," the name for the plant. Bot.
name for the Chicory or Succory group.

Chicory. Eng. for Cichorium.

Cicuta (chi-ku-ta). L. name for Hemlock. Bot. name
for Cowbane group.

Cicutarium (chi-ku-tar-i-um). L. adj., "somewhat
hemlock-like," from cicuta-hemlock; refers to
shape of the leaves.

Ciliaris (si-li-a-ris).

Ciliata (sil-i-a-ta). Both L. adj., from "cilium" (an
eye-lash); long hairs on the margin of a plant or
leaf.

Cineraria (sin-er-a-ri-a). L. "Cineres" (a cinder);
from the ash-coloured down on the underside of the
leaf. Is the gardeners' name for exotic species of
Senecio group.

Cinerea (sin-er-ea). L. "Cineres" (a cinder); *i.e.*, ash-coloured.

Cinquefoil (singk-foil). French. "Cinq" (five); "foil" (a leaf); refers to the number of leaflets that usually form the leaf of the plant. Eng. name for one of the Potentils.

Circeaea (sir-ce-a-e). L. Named after the Enchantress Circe. Bot. name for a group.

Circinatus (sir-cin-a-tus). L. "Circino" (to make round); from the shape of the leaf. Second bot. name, variety Water Rununeulus.

Cirsium (sir-um). L. term used by some botanists for "cnicus."

Cistus (sis-tus). G. name for some shrub. Eng. name for Cistaceæ family.

Cistaceæ (sis-ta-si-e). L. "Cistus" and "aceus" (like). Bot. name for a family which has one group, Rockrose only.

Citrata (sit-ra-ta). L. "Citrus" (a lemon). Second bot. name, variety Watermint.

Cladium (kla-di-um). G. "Clados" (a branch); from its many branches. Bot. name for a group.

Clandestina (klan-des-ti-na). L. adj., "hidden"; from the seeds being hidden in their large coverings. A second bot. name.

Clary (kla-re). L. "Clarus" (clear); is another name for the Wild Sage, and gets this name from the seeds having been put into the eye to clear them by the herbalists of old.

Claytonia (klay-ton-ia). Named after Clayton, an American botanist, who died 1773. Bot. name for a group.

Claw. The "claw" of a petal is the narrow, lengthened base of a petal.

Clavatum (kla-va-tum). L. "Clava." (a club;) from the club-like shape of the spores of the plant. A second bot. name.

Claviculata (kla-vik-u-la-ta). L. name for a "tendril." Second bot. name for Climbing Corydal.

Cleavers (klev-ers). The common name for the Goose-grass, which it gets from the way its many seed vessels, each armed with many tiny hooks, "cleave" to one's clothes.

Clematis (klem-a-tis). G. "Clema" (a vine shoot); from the way the plant grows. Bot. name for a group.

Clinopodium (klin-o-po-di-um). G. "Cline" (a bed); "pous" (a foot). This word was the Greek name for some plant of Umbellate family, and was given because the tufts in which the plant grew were like in shape to the feet of their beds. Second bot. name for Wild Basil.

Cloudberry. Common Eng. name for one of the Rubus group. Said to get this name from its growing on the tops of mountains up among the clouds.

Clove Pink. "Clove," from its scent; "pink," short for Pinkstein; i.e., Penticost, a time when it flowers. Common name for exotic species of the Pink family.

Clover. A.S. "Claefer" (to cleave). Eng. name for a group.

Club Moss. Welsh. "Clob" (a knob); from the club-like shape of the seed vessels. Eng. name for Lycopodium group.

Cnicus (kni-kus). G. "Cnizo" (to prick). Was the

bot. name of a sub-division of the Thistle group, but now disused.

Cochlearia (kok-le-a-ri-a). L. " Cochlear " (a spoon); spoon-like from the shape of the leaf. Bot. name for a group.

Cockle. A corruption of the Gaelic " cogall," name of the plant; usually called " corn cockle," because it flowers with the corn. Eng. name for one of the Lychnis group.

Cock's Foot. Eng. name for Dactylus group.

Codlings and Cream. A common name for Great Willow Herb, because the smell of the flower is like that of boiled apples. Codlin is an old word for apples fit for boiling or baking.

Coenosus (se-no-sus). L. adj., " marshy," i.e., where the plant grows.

Colchicum (kol-chi-kum). Named after Colchis, a province of Asia Minor, where this plant grew abundantly. Bot. name for a group.

Cole or Kole. Saxon " caul," the old name for a cabbage.

Colemani (kol-man-i). Name after Coleman. Second bot. name, variety of Bramble.

Collina (kol-li-na). L. adj., " hilly." A second bot. name.

Colt's Foot. Eng. name for Tussilago group, from the leaf of the plant being like a colt's foot. The leaves are sometimes smoked.

Columbine (kol-um-bine). L. " Columba " (a dove); from the flower spurs being like a group of doves with their heads together.

Columbinum (kol-um-bi-num). L. adj., " like a dove." Second bot. name Long Stalked Geranium.

Columbaria (kol-um-ba-ri-a). L. " Columbarium " (a
dovecote). Second bot. name Small Scabious.

Columnae (kol-um-nae). After Columna, the Italian
botanist, died 1650. Second bot. name Common
Roumulea.

Colza (kol-za). French. " Colza " (the wild cabbage);
a cabbage cultivated for its seed, and from which
Colza oil is got; the refuse is the oil-cake given to
cattle.

Comarum (kom-a-rum). G. " Komaros," name for
the Strawberry tree. Linneus put a plant, now
grouped as Marsh Potentil, into a separate group,
which he named " Comarum."

Comfrey (kum-fre.) L. Is a corruption of " con-
firma " (to establish); refers to the plant being good
for uniting bones. Eng. name for Symphytum
group.

Commixtus (kom-mix-tus). L. adj., " mingling." A
second bot. name, probably applied to plants supposed to be cross-bred.

Communis (kom-mun-is). L. adj., " common." A
very common second bot. name used for sorts of
plants so common as to be unmeaning.

Commutatum (kom-mu-ta-tum). L. adj., " altered."
Second bot. name, variety Heath Galium.

Comosa (ko-mo-sa). L. adj., " hairy." A second bot.
name.

Compactum (kom-pak-tum). L. adj., " compact." A
second bot. name.

Complanatum (kom-pla-na-tum). L. " Complano " (to
make level). A second bot. name.

Compositae (kom-poz-it-e). L. " Compositus " (put
together). A number of little florets put together

form a flower in a dense head, such as the Daisy Thistle, &c. It is the bot. name for the largest family, having in all 41 groups.

Composite (kom-poz-it). Eng. name for above family.

Compressus (kom-pres-sus). L. adj., " pressed." A second bot. name.

Concinus (kon-sin-us). L. adj., " pretty," " neat." A second bot. name.

Condensata (kon-den-sa-ta). L. adj., " thick, dense." Second bot. name.

Conferta (kon-fer-ta). L. adj., " pressed together." A second bot. name.

Confervoides (kon-fer-voi-des). L. "Conferva " (name for some sort of Water Plant); G. " oides " (like). Second bot. name applied to one of the many varieties of the Water Ranunculus.

Confusa (kon-fu-sa). L. adj., " perplexing "; probably as under which group it should be placed. A second bot. name.

Congesta (kon-jest-a). L. adj., " thick." Second bot. name.

Conglomeratus (kon-glom-er-a-tus). L. adj., " crowded together "; *i.e.*, flowers close clustered into a ball. A second bot. name.

Conica (kon-i-ka). L. adj., " cone-shaped." A second bot. name.

Coniferae (kon-if-er-a). L. "Conus " (a cone); "fero " (to bear). Bot. name for the Pine family.

Conium (kon-i-um). G. " A top." The spinning motion of which is like that caused from eating of the plant. Bot. name for the Hemlock group.

Conjungens (kon-jung-ens). L. adj., " united." A second bot. name.

Conjuncta (kon-junk-ta). L. adj., "joined." A
second bot. name.

Conopodium (kon-o-po-di-um). G. "Konos" (a cone);
"pous" (a foot); the flower cup (calyx) being cone-
shaped. Bot. name for a group.

Conopsea (kon-op-sea). G. "Canops" (a gnat).
Second bot. name of Fragrant Orchid.

Consolidus (kon-sol-i-dus). L. adj., "make firm." A
second bot. name.

Conspersus (kon-sper-sus). L. adj., "scattering"; *i.e.*,
its seeds. Second bot. name.

Contorta (kon-tor-ta). L. adj., "powerful." A second
bot. name.

Convallaria (kon-va-la-ri-a). L. "Convallis" (a valley); refers to plant liking low sheltered ground.
Bot. name for a group.

Convexa (kon-veks-a). L. adj., "arched." A second
bot. name.

Convolvulaceæ (kon-vol-vu-la-se-a). L. "Convolvulus" and "aceous" (like). Bot. name Convolvulus family.

Convolvulus (kon-vol-vu-lus). L. "Convolvulo" (to
twine round). Bot. name for Bindweed group.

Conyza (ko-ni-za). G. name for the Inula. Now used
as second bot. name for Ploughman's Spikenard.

Corallina (kor-al-li-na). G. "Korallion" (coral).
Second bot. name applied to the wild variety of
Paeony found on "Steep Holme" Island in the
Severn.

Corallorhiza (kor-al-lo-rhi-za). G. "Korallion" (coral);
"rhiza" (a root); *i.e.*, coral-rooted; refers to the
roots of plant being like branched coral. Bot.
name Coral-root group.

Coral-Root. Eng. name for above group. Also Eng. name for Bulbiferous Bittercress.

Corchorus (kor-ko-rus). Was the old bot. name for the group in which the Jews' Mallow, a double yellow-flowered Japanese shrub, very common in cottage gardens, was placed.

Cordata (kor-da-ta). L. " Cor " (the heart); from the leaves being heart-shaped. A second bot. name.

Cord-Grass. Eng. name for the only Grass in Spartina group.

Cordifolia (kord-i-fol-i-a). L. " Cor " (heart); " folia " (a leaf); from the leaf being heart-shaped. A second bot. name.

Coriander (kor-i-and-er). Eng. rendering of " Corian-drum." See below.

Coriandrum (kor-i-and-rum). G. " Koris " (a bug); from the smell of the leaf when crushed. Bot. name of a group.

Corifolia (kor-i-fol-ia). L. " Korion " (leather); " folia " (a leaf); i.e., leathery-leaved. A second bot. name.

Corm (korm). G. " Kormos " (a stem); is a botanical term for a bulb-like underground stem, not having coats, like the Onion, but solid, as in the Crocus, Gladiolus, &c.

Corn. Gaelic. " Caoran " (berries or seeds); a somewhat common Eng. suffix applied to several plants, as Corn Cockle, &c.

Cornaceæ (kor-na-se-a). L. " Cornus " (name of the tree) and " aceous " (like). Bot. name for Cornel family.

Cornel (kor-nel). An Eng. corruption of L. " Cornus." (See Dogwood.)

Corniculatus (korn-ik-u-la-tus). L. "Cornicula" (a little crow) ; refers to the bird's-claw-like shape of the fruit. Second bot. name for Bird's Foot Trefoil.

Corn Salad. Eng. name for Valerianella group.

Cornus (kor-nus). L. name for Cornel tree. Bot. name for only group of Cornel family.

Cornubiense (kor-nu-bi-en-se). Cornwall put into a L. dress. Second bot. name for Cornish Physosperm.

Coronata (kor-on-a-ta). L. "Corona" (a crown). A second bot. name.

Coronopus (kor-o-no-pus). G. "Koron" (a crow) ; "pous" (foot). Second bot. name for Watercress, "Crowfoot." The translation in Eng. is the common name for one of the Buttercups.

Corrigiola (kor-rij-i-ola). L. "Corrigia" (a strap). Bot. name for Strapwort group.

Corynephorus (kor-i-ne-for-us). G. "Korune" (a club) ; "phoros" (bearing) ; a synonym for group Aira.

Corydal (kor-id-al). Eng. name for Corydalis group.

Corydalis (kor-id-al-is). G. name for the Fumitory. Now used as the name for a group.

Corylifolius (kor-il-i-fol-i-us). L. "Corylus" (the Hazel) ; "folius" (a leaf) ; *i.e.,* Hazel-leaved. A second bot. name.

Corylus (kor-i-lus). L. name for the Hazel. Now applied to Hazel group.

Corymb (kor-imb). L. "Corymbus" (a cluster of flowers). Is a bot. term for a flat-topped cluster of flowers, like that of the Elder, where the stalk of each flower springing low down are longer than that of those higher up, and thus bringing all the flowers to one and the same level.

Corymbiferæ (kor-imb-if-er-a). L. "Corymb" and "fero" (to carry). Bot. name given to a subdivision of Composite family.

Corymbosus (kor-imb-os-us). L. adj., "arranged in corymbs." Second bot. name.

Cotinifolius (ko-ti-ni-fol-i-us). L. name for some plant that gave a purple dye; and "folius" (a leaf); *i.e.*, leaves like those of the "cotinus." A second bot. name.

Cotoneaster (ko-to-ni-as-ter). L. "Cotoneum" (the Quince). Bot. name for a group.

Cotton (kot-n). Is now the name applied to the soft, downy, hair-like substance attached to the seeds of some plants. It is derived from the Arabic "quton," which was their name for the wool of their flocks.

Cotton-Sedge. Eng. name for Eriophorum (G. "wool-bearer,") group Sedge family.

Cotula (kot-u-la). In days of old, for some reason or other, the plant "Stink Mayweed" was by herbalists called Cotula. Now used as second bot. name for that plant.

Cotyledon (kot-i-le-don). G. "Kotuledon" (a hollow vessel); is the future leaf contained in the seed of the plant. Bot. name for a group.

Couch (kowch). Or Quitch. From A.S. "cwice" (quick or living); is the common name for a very troublesome Grass.

Cow Bane. "Bane" is A.S. for "killer." Cowbane is Eng. name for Cicuta group. It is also the common name for the Water Hemlock.

Cow Berry. A common name for Red Whortleberry.

Cow Slip. A.S. " Cu-slyppe " (cowdung). Common name for one of the Primrose group.

Cow Wheat. Eng. name for Melapyrum (G. " black wheat "). Cows are said to like this fodder; sheep do not. The butter of cows fed upon it is said to be very rich and deep yellow colour.

Crab Apple. " Crab," from the Gaelic " craobh " (a tree).

Crack Willow. One of our most common Willows gets this distinguished name because its branches, although pliant and tough, readily " crack " off.

Cracca (krak-ka). G. A corruption of " arachon," the name for some pea plant, but now used as second bot. name for Tufted Vetch.

Crambe (kram-be). G. " Crambe " (kale or cabbage). Bot. name for Seakale group.

Cranberry. Said to be " cranes' berry " because the fruit is ripe about the time these birds arrive. Eng. name for one of the Vaccinum group.

Crane's Bill. A popular name for the Geranium; because Geranium gets its name from G. " geranos " (a crane), and the fruit of the plant is like a crane's bill.

Crassifolius (kras-i-fol-i-us). L. " Crassus " (thick); " folius " (leaf); *i.e.*, thick-leaved. A second bot. name.

Crasulaceæ (kras-u-la-se-a). L. " Crassula " and " aceous " (like). Bot. name for the Crassula family, the whole of which have, more or less, thick succulent leaves.

Crataegus (kra-te-gus). G. " Kratos " (strength);

from the strength of the wood.   Bot. name for
Hawthorn group.

Creeping Jenny. A common name for the Moneywort,
because of its creeping stems.   The name for one
of the Lysmachia group.

Crepis (kre-pis).   G.   "Krepis " (a sandal); from the
shape of the leaf. Bot. name for a group.

Crepiniana (kre-pin-i-an-a).   A second bot. name for
one of the many varieties of the Dog Rose.

Cress.   Eng.   name   for   L.   "criscere ". (to   grow
quickly).   Of Lepidium group.

Crispus (kris-pus).   L. adj., " curled."   A second bot.
name.

Crista-Galli (kris-ta-gal-li).   L.   " Crista " (a crest);
" galli " (of a cock); i.e., cock's comb; refers to
the shape of the Calyx.   Second bot. name for the
Common Rattle.

Cristatus (kris-ta-tus).   L. adj., " crested."   A second
bot. name.

Crithmoides (krith-moi-des).   G.   " Krithe " (barley);
"oides " (like).   Second bot. name Golden Samphire, Inula group.

Crithmum (krith-mum).   G.   " Krithe " (barley); the
fruit of plant being like the seed of the Barley.
Bot. name Samphire group.

Crocus (kro-kus).   G.   " Kroke " (a thread); refers to
the dried stigmas as Saffron.   Bot. name for a
group.

Crocatum (kro-ka-tum).   L. adj., " saffron coloured."
A second bot. name.

Croton (kro-ton).   Name of a foreign group of Spurge
family; cultivated in hot-houses.

Cross Wort.   A common name for one of Gallium

group. Gets its "cross" from both leaves and petals being arranged Maltese-cross way; "wort" (Saxon for plant).

Crow Berry. Eng. name for Empetrum group (see Kraka). The black berries are greedily eaten by crows.

Croweana. Second bot. name for one of the many varieties of Tea-leaved Willow, Salix group.

Crow Foot. Or Buttercup. Is the usual name given to all the members of the Ranunculus group. All of them, except Water Crowfoot, are acrid, and are not eaten by cattle, but when dried and made into hay lose their acridity.

Cruciferæ (kroo-sif-er-a). L. "Crux" (a cross); "fero" (to bear); because the four petals of all the flowers of this family are arranged in the form of the Maltese Cross. This family has 27 groups. Cabbage, Kale, Turnip, Radish, &c., all belong to it.

Cruciata (kroo-si-a-ta). L. adj., "cross-shaped"; hence Eng. name "crosswort" for the plant; also known as Maywort. Second bot. name.

Crus-Galli (krus-gal-li). L. "Crus" (a leg); "galli" of a cock; i.e., Cockspur. Second bot. name of one of Panicum group.

Cryptogams (krip-to-gams). G. "Kruptos" (concealed); "gammos" (marriage); from the organs of fructification not being readily seen. "They have no real flower, neither stamens nor pistils nor true seeds, the fructification consisting of minute granules, called Spores, enclosed in Spore cases, often called capsules."

Cryptogramme (krip-to-gram-me). G. "Kruptos"

(concealed); "gramma" (a line); the lines of fructification not being apparent. Bot. synonym for Allosorus, name of a group.

Cucubalus (ku-ku-ba-lus). From two G. words meaning a noxious weed. Pliny applied it to the Black Nightshade. Now used as second bot. name for one of the Campions, Silene group.

Cucumber (ku-kum-ber). Eng. name from L. "cucumis" (a cucumber), for a vegetable of Gourd family.

Cucurbitaceæ (ku-kur-bit-a-se-a). L. "Cucurbita" (a gourd); and "aceous" (like). Bot. name for Gourd family. The males and females of this family are in separate flowers, either on the same or different plants.

Cudweed. A corruption, probably of cotton-weed, the plants being covered more or less with cottony wool. Eng. name for Gnaphalium group.

Culm (kulm). L. "Culmus" (a stalk). Bot. term more especially used for the stem of Grasses and Sedges.

Cupulifera (ku-pul-if-er-a). L. "Cupula" (a little cup); "fera" (bearer). Is the name of one of the four sub-divisions of the Catkin family. The "cup-bearers" get their name from the little cup in which the fruit rests, as the cup of the Acorn, Filbert, &c.

Currant. A corruption of Corinth, in Greece, whence they were first brought. Is the popular Eng. name for most of the Ribes group.

Cuscuta (kus-ku-ta). Arabic. "Kechout" (the name for the plant). Bot. name Dodder group.

Cuspidatus (kus-pi-da-tus). L. adj.; "somewhat pointed." A second bot. name.

Curta (kur-ta). L. adj., " shortened." A second bot. name.

Cyanus (si-an-us). G. " Cyanos " (blue) ; G. name for the plant. Second bot. name for the Bluebottle or Cornflower.

Cyclamen (sik-la-men). G. " Kuklos " (a circle). Bot. name for a group.

Cymbalaria (sim-bal-ar-i-a). L. adj., " somewhat like a cymbal." Second bot. name Ivy Linaria.

Cyme (sim). I. " Cyma " (sprout of a cabbage). A bot. term for one of the kinds of flowering, where flowers open from below upwards or from the circumference inwards.

Cynanchica (si-nangke-ka). G. name for " Quinsy "; the plant was a supposed remedy for the disease. Second bot. name Squinceywort.

Cynaroideæ (si-na-roi-de-a). G. " Cynara " (a thistle) ; " oides " (like). Is the bot. name for one of the great sub-divisions into which the Composite family is divided.

Cynapium (si-na-pi-um). G. " Kuno " (a dog) ; " apion " (parsley). Second bot. name for Fool's Parsley.

Cynodon (si-no-don). G. " Kuno " (a dog) ; " odon " (a tooth). Bot. name for a group.

Cynoglossum (si-no-glos-sum). G. " Kuno " (a dog) ; " glossum " (a tongue). Bot. name for Hound's Tongue group.

Cynosurus (si-no-su-rus). G. " Kuno " (a dog) ; " aura " (a tail) ; from the shape of the spike, and being fringed on one side only. Bot. name for Dog's Tail group.

Cyperaceæ (si-per-a-se-a). G. " Kupeiros " (a marsh

plant); and " aceous " (like). Bot. name for the Sedge family.

Cyperus (si-perus). G. " Kupris " (Venus), so called from Cyprus, the island where she was born. Bot. name for a group.

Cypripedium (si-pri-pe-di-um). G. " Kupris " (Venus); " podion " (a slipper); from the shape of the flower. Eng. name Lady's Slipper. Bot. name for a group.

Cystopteris (sist-op-ter-is). G. " Kutis " (a bladder); " pteris " (a fern). Bot. name for Bladder-Fern group.

Cytisus (sit-i-sus). L. name for some plant. Now applied as bot. name for Broom group.

Cyphel (si-fel). G. " Kuphos " (bent). Eng. name for Arenaria Cherleri.

D

Dabeoc (St.) (da-bok). St. Dabeoc's Heath, named after the Irish Saint of that name; found only in Ireland, unknown in Great Britain. Dabeocia is a synonym for Menziesia.

Dactylis (dak-til-is). G. " Daktulos " (a finger); from the shape of the panicle. Bot. name for Cock's Foot group.

Dactylon (dak-til-on). G. " Daktulos " (a finger); from its singularly finger-like spikes. Is second bot. name for the only member of Cynodon group.

Daffodil (daf-o-dil). A corruption of G. " asphodel " the name for some lily. Is the well-known Eng. name for plants of the Narcissus group.

Dahlia (da-li-a). Named after Dahl, a Swedish botanist; first introduced from Madrid by Lady Bute in 1789.

Daisy. Corruption of A.S. "daeges eage" (day's eye). Eng. name for the only plant Bellis group.

Dalechamp (da-le-shamp). A French botanist, who died about 1588.

Damascena (dam-a-se-na). L. adj., "of Damascus," as the Damson tree was called. Second bot. name for one of the many varieties of Tea-leaved Willow.

Damson. Eng. corruption of Damascus. The Damascus plum was called "Damson."

Damsonium (dam-son-i-um). L. name for some sort of water plant, but now used as the bot. name for a group of the Alisma family.

Dandelion (dan-di-li-on). Eng. corruption of the French rendering of L. "dens-leonis" (lions' teeth), which it received from the resemblance of the jagged points of its leaf to the teeth of a lion. Eng. name of Taraxicum group.

Danewort. Eng. name for Dwarf Elder, said only to grow where blood has been shed in battle or in murder. It gets "Dane" because wherever the Danes fought there the plant grows abundantly.

Danicus (dan-i-kus). L. "Danae" was the name of a sort of Butchers' Broom. Now used as a second bot. name.

Daphne (daf-ne). G. name of a Nymph, who was changed into a laurel to escape from Apollo. Bot. name for the only group in Daphne family.

Daphnoides (daf-noi-des). G. "Daphne" (see above); "oides" (like); i.e., laurel-like. A second bot. name.

Darnel (dar-nel). Eng. name for a grass of Lolium group; gets its name "Darnel" from an old

French word, "darne" (stupified), from its supposed intoxicating properties.

Dasyphyllum (das-i-fil-lum). G. "Dasu" (thick); "phyllum" (leaf); *i.e.*, thick-leaved. A second bot. name.

Datura (da-tu-ra). A corruption of "tatorah," the Arabic name for the plant. Now Bot. name for a group.

Daucus (daw-kus). G. name for the Carrot. Now bot. name for a group.

Daucoides (daw-koi-des). G. "Daucus" (a carrot); "oides" (like); *i.e.*, carrot-like. A second bot. name.

Deadly Nightshade. See Nightshade.

Dead Nettle. Eng. name for the Lamium group. These are not nettles at all; the true Nettle belongs to quite another family. There are three "Dead Nettles," Red, White and Yellow; are called "dead" because they do not sting; "nettle" because the leaf is like that of the true Nettle.

Dead Tongue. One of the common names for Hemlock Oenanthe, a poisonous plant which paralyses the tongue.

Debilis (deb-il-is). L. adj., "weak." A second bot. name.

Decidua (de-sid-u-a). L. adj., "falling off." A second bot. name.

Decipiens (de-sip-i-ens). L. adj., "deceptive." A second bot. name.

Declinata (de-klin-a-ta). L. adj., "bent downwards." A second bot. name.

Decumbens (de-kum-bens). L. adj., "lying down." A second bot. name.

Deflexus (de-flek-us). L. adj., "bent down." A second bot. name.

Delphinium (del-fin-i-um). G. name for the Dolphin, from the shape of the flower. Bot. name for Larkspur group.

Deltoides (del-toid-es). "Delta" (fourth letter of G. alphabet); and "oides" (like); *i.e.*, triangular. A second bot. name.

Demersum (de-mer-sum). L. adj., "sinking down"; *i.e.*, in water. Second bot. name.

Densiflora (den-si-flo-ra). L. "Densus" (close set); "flora" (a flower). A second bot. name.

Densus (den-sus). L. adj., "close set." A second bot. name.

Dens-Leonis (dens-le-o-nis). L. "Lion's teeth" (see Dandelion).

Dentaria (den-tar-i-a). L. adj., "having teeth"; from the tooth-like scales on the root. Linneus put the Bulbiferous Bittercress into a group called by this name, but now is included in Bittercress group.

Dentata (den-ta-ta). L. adj., "toothed." A second bot. name.

Denticulatum (den-tic-u-la-tum). L. adj., "little-toothed"; *i.e.*, finely toothed. A second bot. name.

Denudatum (de-nud-a-tum). L. adj., "uncovered." Second bot. name.

Deodara (de-o-dar-a). Deodar is the Eng. name for Indian Cedar. It was introduced in 1831 into Britain from India. In the Bombay Presidency there is a minor state named Deodar; if the seed was thence obtained, it may be how the tree came to its name.

Depauperata (de-paw-per-a-ta). L. adj., "impoverished." A second bot. name.

Depressa (de-pres-sa). L. adj., "lying low." A second bot. name.

Derasus (de-ra-sus). L. adj., "rubbed off." A second bot. name.

Deslongchamps (de-long-shamp). A French botanist, who died in 1849.

Devil's-Bit. Eng. name for one of the Scabious; from the root stock ending abruptly, as if bitten off. The story goes that the Devil, annoyed at the many and great uses the plant proved to man, in anger bit the end off.

Dianthus (di-an-thus). G. "Dios" (Jupiter); "anthos" (a flower). Is the bot. name for the Pink group.

Diandrus (di-an-drus). G. "Di" (two); "andros" (man); a term applied by Linneus to plants having only two stamens or male flowers. A second bot. name.

Dichora (di-ko-ra). G. adj., "two-coloured." A second bot. name.

Dicotyledon (di-kot-i-le-don). G. "Di" (two); "cotyledon" (a hollow cup); refers to the two first leaves, which form a cover to the seed of the plant. Bot. name for one of the great divisions into which all plants are divided. All plants which have two lobes in their seeds, i.e., peas, beans, &c., belong to this division.

Didyma (did-i-ma). G. "Didymos" (double); i.e., have two pairs of stamens (males), one pair shorter than the other. A second bot. name.

Diffusus (dif-u-sus). L. adj., " spread out." A second
   bot. name.

Digitalis (dig-it-a-lis). L. adj., " finger-like." Bot.
   name for Foxglove group.

Digitaria (dig-it-ar-ia).

Digitata (dig-it-a-ta). Both L. " digitus " (a finger).
   Second bot. names.

Digraphis (di-graf-is). G. " Di " (two); " graphis "
   (style). Bot. name for a group of Grass family.

Dilatatum (di-la-ta-tum). L. adj., " enlarging." Second
   bot. name.

Dillseed. The seeds of an aromatic plant, used as a
   soothing medicine for children. " Dill " is an old
   word which means " to quiet."

Diœcious (di-esh-i-us). G. " Di " (two); " oikos "
   (house); *i.e.*, when the male and female flowers of
   a plant are each separate in a flower by themselves.
   A common second bot. name.

Dioscorideæ (di-os-kor-i-de-a). After Dioscorides, a G.
   physician, who lived somewhere about the second
   century, and wrote on herbs and their uses. Is the
   bot. name for the Yam family.

Diotis (di-o-tis). G. " Di " (two); " otis " (ears);
   refers to the two ear-like projections at the base of
   the flower and which adhere to the fruit. Bot.
   name for a group.

Diplotaxis (di-plo-tax-is). G. " Diplo " (double);
   " taxis " (row); refers to the double row of seeds.
   Bot. name with some botanists for one of the
   groups.

Dipsaceæ (dip-sa-ke-a). Bot. name for the Teasel
   family.

Dipsacus (dip-sa-kus). G. " Dipsao " (thirst); be-

cause the leaves on the stem, being united, form a
sort of cup in which water is retained, and flies
drowned for the feeding of the plant. Bot. name
for Teasel group of Teasel family.

Disandra (dis-an-dra). See Diandrus.

Discolour (dis-kol-ur). L. adj., "various colours." A
second bot. name.

Dissectum (dis-sekt-um). L. adj., "cut up"; refers
to the leaves being much cut up. A second bot.
name.

Distichia (dis-tik-a). G. "Dis" (two); "stichos"
(rows). A second bot. name.

Dittander (dit-ander). The herbalists' name for the
Lepidium Latifolia; also known as Pepperwort.
Both this plant and another, Origanum Dictamnus,
were known as Dittany—a corruption of Dictamnus. To prevent confusion, apparently, the name
of the Pepperwort was turned to Dittander.

Diurnus (di-ur-nus). L. adj., "by day"; refers to the
time of its flowering to distinguish from those that
flower in the evening. A second bot. name.

Divaricatum (di-var-i-kat-um). L. adj., "spread out."
Second bot. name.

Divergens (di-ver-gens). L. adj., "turning in a different way." A second bot. name.

Diversifolius (di-ver-si-fol-i-us). L. "Diversus"
(different ways); "folius" (leaf). A second bot.
name.

Divisa (di-vi-sa). L. adj., "divided." Second bot.
name.

Divulsa (di-vul-sa). L. adj., "torn asunder." Second
bot. name.

Dock. A.S. " Docce " (name for the plant). Eng. name for the Rumex group.

Dodder. German. " Dotter," name of plant. Eng. name for Cuscuta group. Is an annual parasitical plant; lives chiefly on Furze.

Dog's Tail. Eng. translation of G. " Cynosurus," the name given to a group of the Grass family, the spike being fringed on one side only.

Dog's Mercury. Eng. name for one of the two Mercurys.

Dog-Wood. Eng. name for the Cornel tree. " Dog " has nothing to do with the animal; it is a corruption of A.S. " dags " (a goad or skewer), because wood of this tree was used for making them.

Doronic (dor-on-ik). Eng. rendering of Doronicum.

Doronicum (dor-in-i-kum). Arabic name of plant " durungi " in Latin dress. Bot. name for a group of Composite family.

Dortmanna (dort-man-na). After Dortmann, a Dutch apothecary. Second bot. name of the Water Lobelia.

Domestica (do-mes-tika). L. adj., " belonging to the house." Second bot. name.

Down or Downy. A bot. term when the hairs on a plant are short and soft.

Draba (dra-ba). G. " Drabe " (acrid); refers to the taste of the leaves. Bot. name for a group.

Drop Wort. Eng. name for two plants of different families—(1) Spirea group, Rose family; (2) Water Dropwort, Oenanth group, Umbellate family. The roots of both are knobby. Dropper is the word for a small Tulip bud.

7

Drosera (dros-er-a). G. "Drosos" (dew); from the dew-like drops on the leaves. Bot. name for Sundew group.

Droseraceæ (dros-er-a-se-a). G. "Drosera" and "aceous" (like). Bot. name for Sundew family.

Drupe (droop). L. "Drupae" (an over-ripe olive). Bot. term for soft, fleshy fruit, having hard shelled seed inside.

Dryas (dri-as). G. "Drys" (oak). Bot. name for group.

Dryopteris (dri-op-ter-is). G. "Drys" (oak); "pteris" (fern). Second bot. name for Oak Fern.

Dubius (du-bi-us). L. adj., "doubtful." A second bot. name for many plants.

Duckweed. Eng. name for Lemna group.

Dulcamara (dul-ka-ma-ra). Two L. words. "Dulcis" (sweet); "amarus" (bitter); hence our Bittersweet, because the taste of the bark is first bitter then sweet. Second bot. name Nightshade, Solanum group.

Dumalis (du-mal-is). L. "Dumus" (a bush). Second bot. name.

Dumetorium (du-me-tor-i-um). L. "A copse," where the plant grow. Second bot. name.

Duriscula (du-ris-ku-la). L. adj., "somewhat hard." Second bot. name.

Dutch Rush. Was the name given to one of the Horsetails (equisetum) imported from Holland in days of old, when they were largely used for polishing pots and pans. Then Pewter being in general use, the plant was also known as Pewter wort.

Dwale (dwal). Eng. name for Deadly Nightshade. Dwale was the name given in the 14th century to

a drink composed of different herbs to stupify the
patient when undergoing an operation.

Dyer's Rocket. One of the Eng. names for one of the
Mignonettes, at one time much cultivated on
account of different dyes got from the plant.

Dysenterica (dis-en-ter-i-ka). L. for " dysentry," the
plant being a remedy for that disease. Second bot.
name for Fleabane, Inula group.

E

Ebracteatus (e-brak-te-a-tus). L. " E " (without);
" bractea " (bracts) (which see). A second bot.
name.

Ebulus (e-bul-us). L. name for Dwarf Eldertree; its
second bot. name.

Echinatus (ek-in-a-tus). L. adj., "prickly or rough,"
from G. " echinos " (a hedge-hog). A second bot.
name.

Echioides (ek-i-oi-des). G. " Echinos " (a hedge-hog);
" oides " (like); from the very rough edges of the
leaves. Is the second bot. name for the Ox-tongue.

Echinocloa (ek-in-o-klo-a). G. " Echinos " (a hedge-
hog); " cloa " (grass). Is the group name with
some botanists, in which Cockspur Panicum is
placed.

Echinaspora (ek-in-a-spor-a). G. " Echinos " (a hedge-
hog); " spora " (a seed); from the large spores
covered with acute tubercles. Second bot. name
for a variety of European Quillwort.

Echium (ek-i-um). G. " Echis " (a viper); because the
plant was thought to be a remedy for a viper's
bite. Bot. name for group.

Effusus (ef-fuz-us). L. adj., "spread out." A second
bot. name.

Eglantaria (eg-lan-tar-ia). L. adj., formed from Eglan-
tine, the old Eng. name for the Sweet Briar, but
Milton applied it to the Honey Suckle. A second
bot. name.

Elæagnaceæ (e-la-ajna-si-a). G. "Elæagnos" and
"aceous" (like). Bot. name for a family.

Elæagnus (e-la-aj-nus). G. "Alaiagnos" (name of
some unknown marsh plant). Eng. rendering of
the name of the family.

Elatinaceæ (e-lat-in-a-si-a). G. "Elatine" and
"aceous" (like). Bot. name for a family.

Elatine (e-la-tin). G. "Elatine" (name of some unknown plant). Bot. name of a group. Eng. name
for a family.

Elatior (e-lat-i-or).

Elatius (e-lat-i-us). L. adj., "higher." A second bot.
name.

Elder. A.S. "Ellarn" (the kindler); because its
hollow branches were used to blow up the fire.
Eng. name for a group.

Elecampane (el-kam-pan). A corruption of French
"enule campane." The name for one of the Inula
group.

Elegans (ele-gans). L. adj., "elegant." A second
bot. name.

Eleocharis (ele-o-karis). G. "Heleo" (a marsh);
"charis" (delight); from where the plant delights
to grow. A first bot. name used by some botanists
for some of Scirpus group.

Eleogiton (ele-o-ji-ton). G. "Heleo" (a marsh);

"giton" (bred); *i.e.*, grows there. Synonym for first bot. name Floating Scirpus.

Elisma (el-is-ma). See Alisma.

Elm. Eng. name for Ulnus group. Apparently this tree is known by the same name in all languages.

Elodea (e-lo-dia). G. "Heledos" (growing in a marsh). Bot. name for a group; used also as a second bot. name.

Elongata (e-long-a-ta). L. adj., "elongated." A second bot. name.

Elymus (al-e-mus). After Elyma, a Greek town, where the plant was common. Bot. name for Lymegrass group.

Embryo (em-bri-o). G. "Embryon" (a fetus). A bot. term for the rudiment of the plant contained in the seed.

Emersistylus (e-mer-sis-ti-lus). L. "Emersus" (emerging); "stylus" (a stem). Second bot. name for one of the many varieties of Bramble.

Empetraceæ (em-pet-ra-si-a). Bot. name for Empetrum family.

Empetrum (em-pet-rum). G. "En" (in); "petrum" (a rock); grows in rocky places. Bot. name for Crowberry group, the only one of the Empetrum family.

Enchanter's Nightshade. Eng. name for one of Circaea group. The enchanter, or rather enchantress, was Circe, who by her enchantments turned all Ulysses's companions into swine, but Ulysses was immune by virtue of the herb "moly," which Mercury had given to him.

Endive (en-div). From French "endive" (a salad).

Is. the Eng. name of the cultivated variety of the
Wild Chicory.

Endogens (en-do-jens). G. "Endon" (within); "gen-
nao" (produce). Is a bot. term for those plants
like Palms, Grasses, Rushes, &c., whose growth
takes place from within; *i.e.*, Monocotyledons; or
one-lobed.

Endymion (en-dim-i-on). G. name for Sunset personi-
fied, and with whom the Moon is in love. A
synonym for the first bot. name the Bluebell.

Enodium (e-no-dium). L. "E" (without); "nodus"
(a knot). Synonym for first bot. name Purple
Molinia, Grass family.

Ensifolia (en-si-fol-ia). L. "Ensis" (a sword);
"folia" (a leaf); *i.e.*, sword-leafed. A second bot.
name.

Epigeios (epi-je-os). G. "Epi" (on); "geios" (the
earth). A second bot. name.

Epilinum (epi-li-num). G. "Epi" (on); "linum"
(flax); from the plant, a parasite, living on the
Flax. Second bot. name for Flax Dodder, Cuscuta
group.

Epilobe (epi-lob). Eng. for Epilobium.

Epilobium (epi-lo-bium). G. "Epi" (on); "lobos" (a
pod); because the flower as if growing out of the
pod. Bot. name for the Epilobe group.

Epipactis (epi-pak-tis). G. name for one of the Helle-
bores. Now used as bot. name of a group.

Epipogum (epi-po-gum). G. "Epi" (upwards);
"pogum" (the beard); because the flower grows
with its "lip" upwards. Bot. name for a group.

Epithymum (epi-thi-mum). G. "Epi" (on); "Thy-
mum" (Thyme); was the G. name for the Dodder,

a parasitical plant that lives on other plants, among others on the Thyme. Is now second bot. name for Lesser Dodder.

Equisetaceæ (ek-wi-se-ta-si-e). L. "Equisetum" (horse-hair); "aceous" (like). Bot. name for Equisetum; more commonly known as Horsetail family.

Equisetum (ek-wi-se-tum). L. "Equis" (a horse); "setum" (a thick hair, like those found in the tail). Bot. name for a group commonly called Horsetails.

Erecta (e-rek-ta). L. adj., "erect." A very common second bot. name.

Erica (e-ri-ka). The name for "heath" both in G. and L. Bot. name for a group of Heath family.

Ericaceæ (e-ri-ka-si-a). G. "Erike" (heather); "aceous" (like). Bot. name for the Heath family.

Ericetorium (e-rik-et-o-rum). L. adj., "somewhat like heath." Second bot. name.

Erigeron (e-rij-e-ron). G. "Eri" (early); "geron" (an old man); from the grey look of the down on the seed. Bot. name for a group.

Eriocarpa (e-ri-o-car-pa). G. "Erion" (wool); "carpos" (fruit). Second bot. name.

Eriocauleæ (er-e-o-kaw-le). G. "eriocaulon" and L. "aceous" (like). Bot. name for Eriocaulon family.

Eriocaulon, (er-i-o-kaw-lon). G. "Erion" (wool); "caulon" (stem); from the downy stems of the plants. Bot. name for a group.

Eriophorum (e-re-o-fo-rum). G. "Erion" (wool); "phoro" (bearer). Bot. name for Cotton Sedge group.

Erodium (e-ro-di-um). G. name for a Heron. Bot. name for a group of Geranium family, because the fruit of the plant resembles a Heron's beak.

Erophila (e-ro-fil-a). G. " Ero " (spring); " phila " (a lover); synonym by some botanists of Draba (which see).

Erraticus (er-rat-ik-us). L. adj., " erratic." A second bot. name.

Erucifolia (e-ru-ki-fol-ia). L. " Eruca " (a caterpillar); " folia " (a leaf). Second bot. name Narrow-leaved Senecio.

Eryngium (e-rin-ji-um). G. " Erygien " (eructation); plant a remedy for flatulence. Bot. name for a group.

Eryngo (e-rin-go). Eng. rendering of Eryngium.

Erysimum (e-ri-si-mum). G. " Eruo " (to draw up); *i.e.*, to blister. Bot. name for a group.

Erythræa (er-ith-ra-a). G. adj., " red "; from the colours of the flowers. Bot. name Centaury group.

Erythrospermum (er-ith-ro-sper-mum). G. "Erutheros" (red); " spermum " (seed). Second bot. name for one of the four varieties of the Dandelion.

Escallonias (es-kal-lo-ni-as). Belonging to the Saxifrage family.

Escholtzia (esh-sholt-se-a). Are Californian plants of Poppy family.

Esula (es-u-la). Herbalists' name for plant; a corruption of its then bot. name, G. " pityusa " (a pine); now a second bot. name.

Euonymus (u-on-i-mus). After Euonyme, mother of the Furies, the berries being poisonous. Bot. name Spindletree group.

Eupatorium (u-pa-to-re-um). After Eupator, King of
Pontus, who introduced the plant as a medicine.
Bot. name Eupatory group.

Eupatory (u-pa-tor-e). Eng. rendering of Eupatorium.

Euphorbia (u-for-be-a). After Euphorbus, physician to
Juba, king of Mauritania, who first used the plant.
Bot. name for Spurge group.

Euphorbiaceæ (u-for-be-a-se-a). " Euphorbia " and
" aceous " (like). Bot. name Spurge family.

Euphrasia (u-fra-si-a). G. for " delight." Bot. name
Eyebright group.

Europaeus (u-ro-pe-us). Europe in Latin dress. A
second bot. name.

Exacum (egz-a-cum). L. "Exacuo" (to make pointed).
Used as first bot. name.

Excelsior (ek-sel-si-or). L. adj., " more lofty." A
second bot. name.

Exigua (eks-ig-ua). L. adj., " small or mean." A
second bot. name.

Eximium (eks-im-i-um). L. adj., " rare." A second
bot. name.

Exogens (eks-o-jens). G. " Exo " (outside); " gen-
nao " (to produce); plants which grow by additions
to the outside of last year's ring of wood, as in the
Oak, Ash, Elm, &c. These are Dicotyledons
(which see).

Extensa (eks-ten-sa). L. adj., " stretched out." A
second bot. name.

Eye-Bright. Eng. name for Euphrasia, because an
infusion of the plant was a good eye-wash, made
them bright and clear.

F

Fabaria (fa-be-ri-a). L. adj., "bean-like," from "faba" (the horse-bean). A second bot. name.

Fagopyrum (fa-go-pi-rum). G. "Phegos" (beech); "pyros" (wheat); from the shape of the seed being like the beech-nut. Used by some as either a first or second bot. name for one of the Polygonums (see Buckwheat).

Fagus (fa-gus). L. name for "Beech-tree." Bot. name for Beech group.

Falcatus (fal-ka-tus). L. adj., "scythe-shaped." A second bot. name.

False Brome. Eng. name for Brachypodium group, Grass family.

False Oats. Eng. name for the Arrhenatherum group, Grass family.

Farfara (far-far-a). L. name of plant. Second bot. name for Colt's Foot.

Farinosa (far-i-no-sa). L. adj., "very meal-like." Second bot. name applied to several plants having a mealy-like look.

Fascicularis (fas-sik-u-lar-is). L. adj., "anything carried in bundles, as hay, &c." A second bot. name.

Fastigatus (fas-tij-a-tus). L. adj., "sloping to a point." Second bot. name Lombardy Poplar, from the way the tree grows up to a point.

Fatua (fat-u-a). L. adj., "foolish or silly." A second bot. name.

Featherfoil. *i.e.,* Feather-leaved; "foil" (a contraction of L. word for a leaf). Eng. name for the Water Violet.

Fedia (fe-di-a). Linneus' name for Valerianella group.

Fennel. A.S. "Feonel," from the L. "foeniculum." Eng. name for Foeniculum group.

Fennica (fen-nek-a). A second bot. name for a variety of Beam tree.

Fern. A.S. "Fearn." Eng. name for one of the families of Cryptogamic plants. Among the Celts, the Fearn was looked on as a sacred plant. The seeds, being invisible, made those who carried them in their pocket also invisible.

Ferruginous (fer-ru-ji-nus). L. adj., "rust coloured." Second bot. name.

Fescue (fes-ku). Eng. rendering of Festuca, the bot. name for one of the Grass groups.

Festucaceum (fes-tu-ka-se-um). L. adj., "like the festuca." Second bot. name.

Feverfew. A.S. "Feferfuge," from L. "febrifuga"; i.e., fever dispeller. "Few" is merely a corruption of L. "fuga." Eng. name for Chrysanthemum Parthenium.

Fibichia (fib-ich-ia). A synonym used by some for first bot. name Cynodon, of a group Grass family.

Ficaria (fik-ar-ia). L. adj., "fig-like"; from the shape of the roots. A second bot. name.

Ficifolium (fik-i-fol-i-um). L. "Ficus" (a fig); "folium" (a leaf); i.e., "fig-leaved." A second bot. name.

Field Madder. See Madder.

Fig Wort. Eng. name for Scrophularia nodosa; gets its name from the fig-like shape of its tubers.

Filago (fil-a-go). L. "Filium" (a thread); from the thread-like hairs which cover the plant. Bot. name for a group.

Filament. Bot. term for stalk which carries seed vessels of male flower.

Filices (fil-e-ses). L. " Filix " (a fern). Bot. name for Fern family.

Filifolium (fil-e-fol-i-um). L. " Filum " (a thread); " folium " (a leaf). A second bot. name.

Filiforma (fil-e-for-ma). L. " Filum " (a thread); " forma " (shaped). A second bot. name.

Filipendula (fil-e-pen-du-la). L. " Filum " (a thread); " pendula " (hanging by); refers to its tubers hanging down as if by threads. A second bot. name.

Filix-Foemina (fi-lix-fe-mi-na). L. " Filix " (a fern); " foemina " (a female). Second bot. name for Lady Fern, Spleenwort group.

Filix-Mas (fi-lik-mas). L. " Filix " (a fern); " mas " (male). Second bot. name Male Fern, Aspidium group.

Filmy-Fern. Eng. translation of bot. name Hymenophyllum (G. " hymen " (a membrane); " phyllum " (a leaf)); from its filmy leaves. Name of a group, Fern family.

Fiorin-Grass (fi-o-rin). Eng. name for one of the Agrostis group.

Fir. A.S. " Furh " (name of the tree). Is the Eng. name for trees of Abies group, Pine family.

Fissus (fis-sus). L. adj., " cleft." A second bot. name.

Fissifolius (fis-si-fo-li-us). L. " Fissus " (cleft); " folius " (a leaf); *i.e.*, cleft-leaved. A second bot. name.

Fistulosa (fis-tu-lo-sa). L. " Fistula " (a pipe); " osa " (suffix meaning " full of "); *i.e.*, hollow through-

out, as the leaf and stem of an onion. A second
bot. name.

Flabellatus (flab-el-la-tus). L. "Flabellum" (a fan);
i.e., fan-like; from the leaf being fan or wedge
shaped. Second bot. name.

Flag. Welsh. "Llac." Is the Eng. name for two
different plants, Yellow Flag (an Iris) and Sweet
Flag, Acorus group.

Flammula (flam-mu-la). L. "A small flame"; refers
to the redness caused by the leaves on the skin.
A second bot. name.

Flavum (fla-vum).

Flavescens (fla-ves-ens).

Flavescum (fla-ves-kum). L. adj., all three meaning
"yellow," but in varying degrees. Second bot.
names.

Flavicornis (fla-vi-cor-nis). L. "Flavus" (yellow);
"cornis" (horned). Second bot. name for variety
of Dog Violet.

Flax. A.S. "Fleax." Eng. name for Linaceæ
family, and also one of its groups.

Flea Bane. "Bane" is A.S. for "killer." There
are two Flea-banes—one belongs to Inula group;
the other to Erigeron.

Flexile (fleks-il). L. adj., "bent." A second bot.
name.

Flexuosa (fleks-u-osa). L. adj., "bending alternate
ways." Second bot. name.

Flixweed. Eng. name for Sisymbrium Sophia. Flix
means "flux." The seeds were used for dysentry.
So highly did the herbalists value this plant that
they called it "The Wisdom (Sophia) of the Surgeons." Hence its second bot. name.

Floribundus (flo-ri-bun-dus). L. "Flora" (flowers); "abundus" (many). A second bot. name.

Flos-Cuculi (flos-kuk-u-li). L. "Flos" (a flower); "cuculi" (of the Cuckoo). A rather common second bot. name given to plants that flower when the Cuckoo is with us.

Fluitans (flu-i-tans). L. adj., "floating on water." A second bot. name.

Fluviatillis (flu-vi-at-il-lis). L. adj., "belonging to a river"; applied usually to plants growing in streams. Second bot. name.

Fœtida (fet-i-da). L. adj., "stinking"; refers to the smell of the plant. A second bot. name. In the case of the Roastbeef plant—an Iris—the qualifying adjective is in the superlative "foetidissima."

Fœniculum (fen-ik-u-lum). L. word for "hay," because the smell of the leaf resembles that of hay. Bot. name for Fennel group.

Fœnisecii (fen-is-e-ci). L. word for "hay harvest." Used as second bot. name for a variety Broad Shield Fern.

Fontana (fon-ta-na). L. adj., "growing by a spring." A second bot. name.

Fool's-Parsley. Eng. name for Aethusa group. Although somewhat like, only fools would mistake it for real Parsley, hence its name.

Fox Glove. Eng. name for Digitalis group. Fox is a corruption of "Folks"; i.e., the "Good Folk," the Fairies. It is their special flower. The bending of the plant tells of a supernatural person's presence, to whom the plant pays homage.

Fox Tail. Eng. translation of the G. name Alopecurus, of one of the Grass groups.

Fragaria (fra-ga-ri-a). L. "Fragrant" was their name for our Strawberry. Is now the bot. name for Strawberry group.

Fragariastrum (fra-ga-ri-as-trum). L. "Fragaria" (a strawberry); "astrum," when added to a L. word, means "like but not the same thing." A second bot. name.

Fragiferum (fra-gi-fer-um). L. "Fragia" (a strawberry); "ferum" (bearing). A second bot. name.

Fragalis (fra-ja-lis). L. adj., "fragile." A second bot. name.

Frangula (fran-gu-la). L. "Frango" (to break); formerly Frangula was the name for the Alder. It is now second bot. name for Alder Buckthorn.

Frankenia (frank-en-ia). After Franken, a Swedish botanist, who died 1661. Bot. name for a group.

Frankeniaceæ (frank-en-ia-se-e). L. "Frankenia" and "aceous" (like). Bot. name for the family.

Fraxinus (fraks-in-us). L. name for the Ash. Bot. name Ash group.

Frigida (frij-id-a). L. adj., "cold." A second bot. name.

Fritillaria (frit-e-la-ri-a). L. "Fritillus" (a dice-box); because a dice-box often goes with a chequer-board, and the blossom is checkered with lines like a chequer-board. Bot. name for Fritillary group.

Fritillary (frit-e-la-re). Eng. name for above.

Frog Bit. A literal translation of second bot. name, "morsus-ranae," a plant—the only one—of Hydrocharis group.

Frog Orchis. A more popular name for Green Habenaria, Orchid family.

Frondosa (frond-osa). L. adj., "full of leafy branches." Second bot. name.

Fructifera (fruk-tif-era). L. "Fructi" (fruit); "fera" (bearer); *i.e.*, fertile. Second bot. name.

Fruiticosus (fru-ti-ko-sus). L. adj., "very bushy"; from L. "frutex" (a bush). Second bot. name.

Fruticulosa (fru-te-ku-lo-sa). L. adj., "bushy little shrub." Second bot. name.

Fuchsia (few-she-a). After Fuchs, a German botanist, who died 1565.

Fuller's Herb. Another name for Soapwort.

Fullonum (fool-o-num). L. "Fullo" (a fuller). Second bot. name for the cultivated variety of the Wild Teasel. Fullers use the heads of Teasels to raise the nap of cloth.

Fumaria (few-ma-ri-a). L. "Fumus" (smoke); from the smell of the plant. Bot. name for a group.

Fumariaceæ (few-ma-ri-a-se-e). L. "Fumaria" and "aceous" (like). Bot. name Fumitory family.

Fumitory (few-mi-tur-e). Eng. name for a group and of a family.

Fungus (fung-gus). L. word for Mushroom. They are plants of Cryptogams class, and have no Chlorophyll. Mushrooms, Toadstools, &c., belong to this family.

Fuscus (fus-kus). L. adj., "dark or swarthy." A second bot. name.

Fusco-Ater. L. "Fusco" (dark); "ater" (black). A second bot. name.

Furze (furz). A.S. "Fyrs" (name of plant). Eng. name for Ulex group.

G

Gagea. After Gage, the botanist, who died 1820. A group name.

Galanthus (ga-lan-thus). G. "Gala" (milk); "anthus" (flower). Bot. name for Snowdrop group.

Gale (gale). Dutch "gagel" (name of the plant). Eng. name for Myrica group.

Galericulata (gal-e-rik-u-la-ta) L. adj., "having a small skull-cap." Second bot. name for Common Skull-Cap.

Galeobdolon (gal-e-ob-do-lon). G. "Gale" (a weasel); "bdolon" (bad smell from the weasel-like smell of the flower). Second bot. name of Yellow Archangel or Yellow Dead Nettle, Labium group.

Galeopsis (gal-e-op-sis). G. "Gale" (a weasel); "opsis" (like); from the tip of the flower being like the snout of a weasel. Bot. name for a group.

Galingale (gal-in-gale). Eng. name for one of Cyperus group.

Galium (ga-le-um). G. "Gala" (milk); the plants were formerly used for curdling milk. Bot. name for a group.

Galii (ga-li). A synonym for bot. name of Clove-scented Broomrape, a parasitic plant said to grow on Galiums only.

Gallicia (gal-lish-ia). L. "Gallia" (the name for France). A second bot. name for some plants found in the Channel Islands.

Gallicoides (gal-lish-oi-des). L. "Gallica"; G. "oides" (like). Second name for one of Field Roses.

Gang-Flower. Another name for Milkwort, so called

8

from blossoming during " gang " (A.S. "walk-ing ") week, or Rogation week, when parish boundaries are walked round.

Garlic. The popular name for plants of Allium group; from A.S. " gar " (a spear); " leac " (a leek)..

Gastridium (gas-tri-de-um). G. " A little belly "; from the small swelling at base of spikelets. Bot. name Nitgrass group.

Gean (geen). From French " guigne " (fruit of Wild Cherry).

Gemilla (jem-il-la). L. " Gemillus " (twins); because two clusters grow on one stalk. Second bot. name.

Gemmifera (jem-mif-era). L. " Gemma " (a bud); " fero " (to bear). Second bot. name.

Gemmipara (jem-mip-ara). L. " Gemma " (bud); " pario " (produce). A second bot. name.

Genevensis (jen-ev-en-sis). Latinized form " of Geneva." Second bot. name.

Geniculatus (je-nik-u-la-tus). L. adj., " having knots." Second bot. name.

Genista (je-nis-ta). Celtic " Gen " (a shrub). Bot. name for a group.

Gentian (jen-shi-an). Eng. for Gentiana.

Gentiana (jen-shi-a-na). After Gentius, King of Illyria, who brought these plants into medical use. Bot. name for group.

Gentianacæ (jen-shi-an-a-se-e). L. " Gentiana " and " aceous " (like). Bot. name for a family.

Gentilis (jen-til-is). L. adj., " descended from the same ancestor." Second bot. name.

Geraniaceæ (je-ra-ni-a-se-e). G. " geranos " (a crane); L. " aceous," (like). Bot. name of a family.

Geranium (je-ra-ni-um). G. "geranos" (a crane); because the fruit of the plant is like a crane's bill. Bot. name group.

Geraniodes (je-ra-ni-oi-des). G. adj., "Geranium-like." Second bot. name.

Gerardi. After Gerard, an English botanist, who died 1612. A second bot. name.

Germander (jer-man-der). Corruption of Italian "Calmandrea." Eng. name for Teucrium group. Was held in great repute by all herbalists. Once used, in Jersey, instead of hops.

Germanicum (jer-man-ik-um). L. form of "Germanic." Second bot. name.

Geum (je-um). G. "Geuo" (a pleasant smell); from the aromatic root. Bot. name Avens group.

Gibba (gib-ba). L. adj., "humped" (having a swelling somewhere). A second bot. name.

Giganteus (ji-gan-te-us). L. adj., "gigantic." A second bot. name.

Gilliflower (jil-le-flour). A corruption, through Italian, of G. Kaurophyllon (a clove), because the smell of flower or root was like that of the Clove. An old Eng. name applied to many different flowers, but now given to the Common Stock.

Gipsy Wort. Formerly known as the Egyptian's herb, because "the rogues and runnegates, which call themselves Egyptians, and doe color themselves black with this herbe." Is the Eng. name for the Lycopus Europeaus.

Githago (gith-a-go). Probably a herbalists' name for the group to which the Corn Cockle belongs. The Latins had a plant which they called Gith, but now unknown.

Glabrum (gla-brum). L. adj., " without hairs "; *i.e.*, smooth. A second bot. name. In its English (?) form the adj. " glabrous." is often used in description of plants where " smooth " would be more understandable of the people.

Gladdon (glad-don). A corruption evidently of " gladyne," as it was called in 14th century. Is another name for Roastbeef plant—one of the Iris family.

Gladiolus (glad-i-o-lus). L. name for a short sword; refers to the shape of the leaf. Bot. name for a group.

Glandulosus (glan-du-lo-sus). L. adj., " full of kernals." Second bot. name.

Glass-Wort. The common name for Marsh Samphire. It grows in salt marshes, and contains a large quantity of an impure soda, which was extracted and used in-making glass, hence its name.

Glaucium (glaw-se-um). G. adj., " bluish-grey." Bot. name for a group of Poppy family, and of which Sea Poppy is the only member. The colour of the leaves accounts for the name given to the group.

Glaucus (glaw-kus). G. adj., " bluish-grey." A second bot. name for many plants. In describing plants having this colour, some writers use " glaucous " when bluish-grey would be better in every way.

Glaucophyllia (glaw-ko-fil-lia). G. " Glaukos " (bluish grey); " phyllia " (leaves); from the colour of the leaf. Second bot. name.

Glaux (glawks). This is the same as " glaucium," but being used as a group name, is spelt differently.

Glechoma (glek-oma). G. name for someone of the

mints. Now used as second bot. name for Ground
Ivy. Linneus used it as first bot. name for a
group for this plant.

Globe Flower. Eng. name for Trollius, because of the
flower's shape.

Globosum (glo-bo-sum). L. adj., "round like a ball."
Second bot. name.

Globulifera (glo-bu-lif-era). L. adj., "globe-bearer."
Second bot. name.

Glomerata (glom-er-a-ta). L. adj., "formed into a
ball." Second bot. name.

Glume (glewm). A bot. term for husk or covering of
the seed vessels of the Grasses.

Glutinosa (glew-te-no-sa). L. adj., "gluey." A second
bot. name.

Glyce (gli-se). G. "Glukus" (sweet). Used by some
as first bot. name for Sweet Alyssum.

Glyceria (gli-se-re-a). G. "Glukus" (sweet). Used
by some as first bot. name for several of the Poa
group.

Glycyphyllon (gli-se-fil-lon). G. "Glyse" (sweet);
"phyllon" (leaf). Second bot. name Milk Vetch,
Astragal group.

Gnaphalium (naf-al-i-um). G. name for some downy
plant used for stuffing pillows. Bot. name Cudweed group.

Goat's Beard. Translation of Tragapogon. Bot.
name Meadow Salsify.

Gold of Pleasure. Eng. name for Camelina Sativa,
which is cultivated for the oil of its seeds.

Golden Rod. A translation of "virga" (a twig);
"aurea" (golden). The second bot. name of the
plant. It was sold for half-a-crown an ounce by

herb women in Queen Elizabeth's days, as long
as it was imported, but when it was discovered to
be a home plant, it was discarded and of no value.

Goldilocks. Two different plants have this Eng. name.
The reason for the Eng. name is clear in the case
of Auricomus, but not so in the case of the other,
Aster Lionsyris.

Good King Henry. Is the Eng. name of one of the
Goosefoots. It is a good example of the pitfalls
in finding out how plants have come by their names.
Its second bot. name is Bonus Henricus. The
" Bonus " (good) was given to distinguish it from
a poisonous (" Malus ") Henricus plant. Linneus
evidently took the plant name from the Germans,
who called it *Heinrich,* and Latinized it into *Henricus.* This, when translated into English, became
Henry, as if it were a Christian name. Grimm
says " Heinrich " is not a Christian name. It is
a German word for what we in English call goblin.
To make confusion worse confounded, someone has
put in a " King," and the Good Goblin becomes
Good King Henry.

Goodyera. After Goodyear, a Hampshire botanist.
Bot. name for a group Orchid family.

Gooseberry. Eng. name for a well-known fruit. The
bird goose has nothing to do with its name; it is
more likely a corruption of its second name, L.
" Grosslaria," from " grossus " (an unripe fig).

Goose Foot. Eng. translation of the bot. name Chenopodium.

Goose Grass. Eng. name for one of the Galium group,
and so-called because geese are said to do well on
the plant, which is not a grass at all.

Gorse (gors). A.S. "Gorst" (waste ground); where
the plant is usually found. See Furze.

Gothica (goth-ik-a). Latinized form " of Goths "; *i.e.*,
Sweden. Second bot. name.

Gourd. L. "Cucurbita," through Old French "gou-
hourde." Is Eng. name for Cucurbitaceæ
family.

Gout Weed. Evidently from its second bot. name,
Podagraria, which is G. for gout.

Gracilis (gas-il-is). L. adj., "thin or slender." A
second bot. name.

Gracilentem (gras-il-en-tem). L. adj., "graceful
habit." Second bot. name.

Gramineæ (gram-in-e-e). L. "Gramin" (grass).
Bot. name for Grass family. Also used as second
bot. name.

Grammites (gram-mi-tes). G. "Grammi" (a line);
i.e., marked with lines. Bot. name for a group.
Only found in Jersey.

Grape-Hyacinth. Eng. name for Muscari Racemosum;
called "grape" because the flowers cluster like a
bunch of grapes.

Grass of Parnassus. Is not a grass. It belongs to
Saxifrage family. Gets its name from having been
first found on Mount Parnassus in Greece.

Grass-Wrack (rak). This is not a grass in the botanic
sense, but both leaves and flowers are grass-like.
Gets "wrack" from French "varech" (seaweed),
which the plant really is.

Greek-Valerian (va-le-ri-an). Eng. name for the only
Polemonium, but why called Valerian, seeing it
does not belong to that group, is not clear. Mis-
named by someone.

Greenweed. Common name for Dyer's Genitsa. Johns, in his " Flowers of the Fields," says about this plant: "The upper branches are destitute of thorns, and produce leafy clusters of yellow flowers, which (like some other yellow flowers belonging to this natural order) are remarkable for turning green in drying." This accounts for the "green."

Grandifolia (grand-i-fol-ia). L. "Grandis" (large); "folia" (leaves); i.e., big-leaved. A second bot. name.

Granulata (gran-u-la-ta). L. adj., "small-seeded." A second bot. name.

Graveolens (gra-ve-o-lens). L. adj., "strong-smelling." Second bot. name for Wild Celery.

Greenlandica (-ik-a). "Of Greenland" in Latin dress. Second bot. name.

Gromwell (grom-el). Celtic. "Graum" (a seed); "mil" (a stone); the seeds being very stony, contain a lot of flint. Eng. name for bot. name of group, Litho (stone) spermum (seed).

Grossularia (gros-su-la-ri-a). L. "Grossulus" (a small unripe fig). Second bot. name for the Gooseberry.

Ground-Ivy. Eng. name for Nepeta Glechoma. It creeps over the ground, killing all the grass; this may account for the "Ivy" of its name. On account of its bitter property, before hops became common, it was used in the making of beer; hence one of its many names, Ale-hoof.

Ground-Pine. A literal translation of its second bot. name, Chamaepitys.

Groundsel. The common name for a well-known

garden weed. Is a good example of how one mis-
placed letter (in this case an "r") can lead to a
wrong meaning being given for the name of a
plant. For a long time Groundsel was said to
mean "ground-swallower," from its A.S. name,
"grunde-swelge." Now it is found that the
proper spelling of the A.S. word is "gunde-
swelge," *i.e.*, "matter or pus-swallower," a more
reasonable explanation, seeing that Groundsel was
used by herbalists for diseases of the eye.

Gelder-Rose (gel-der). Eng. name for Viburnum
Opulus, because it was introduced from the province of Gelderland, Holland.

Guttatum (gut-ta-tum). L. adj., "spotted." A second
bot. name.

Gymnadenia (jim-na-de-ni-a). G. "Gumnos" (naked);
"aden" (a gland); because it is not covered in a
pouch. A first bot. synonym for some of the
Habenaria group.

Gymnogramma (jim-no-gram-ma). G. "Gumnos"
(naked); "gramma" (a line); because the line of
capsules are not covered. A synonym for first bot.
name Grammitis group, Fern family.

H

Habenaria (hab-en-ar-ia). L. "Habena" (a strap);
because the lip of the flower looks like a strap.
Bot. name of a group, Orchid family.

Hair Grass. Eng. name for one of Aira group.

Halorageae (hal-or-aj-e-e). G. "Alos" (the sea).
Bot. name for Marestail family. The plants of this
family are aquatic.

Haloscias (hal-os-ki-as). G. "Alos" (the sea). Is a
synonym for Ligusticum group.

Hamulata (ha-mul-a-ta). L. adj.; "little hooked." A
second bot. name.

Hardheads. Common name for Knapweed; plants of
Centaurea group.

Hare Bell. Eng. name for one of Campanula group.
It is the true Blue-bell of Scotland. Sometimes
spelt Hairbell, which seems to be more correct.

Hare's Ear. Eng. name for two plants belonging to
different families. One belongs to Erysium group,
the other to the Buplever group.

Hare's Foot. A literal translation of second bot. name
Lagopina. G. "Lago" (a hare); "pous" (a
foot).

Hare's Tail. A translation of bot. name for group
Lagurus. G. "Lago" (a hare); "urus" (a
tail).

Hart's Tongue. Eng. name for one of Scolopendrium
group; from the shape of the frond.

Hartwort. Eng. name for Tordylium group.

Hautboy (ho-boy). Eng. name for a variety of Strawberry; Hautboy, the name for a musical instru-
ment, is derived from French "haut" (high),
"bois" (wood).

Hawkbit. Eng. name for Leontodon group.

Hawk's Beard. Eng. name given by some to plants
of Crepis group.

Hawkweed. Eng. name for Hieracium group. So
named, according to herbalists of old, because the
old hawks were in the habit of using the juice of
these plants to strengthen the sight of their young.
A more likely derivation is, I think, the following:

The Greeks had an eye-salve called "Hierakion," which probably took its name from the eyes of hawks being used in its making, and as the juice of these plants was perhaps one of the ingredients. The name of the salve was also given to the plant.

Hawthorn. Eng. name for Crataegus group. "Haw" is a corruption of A.S. "haga" (a hedge); so the word means the "hedge-thorn."

Hastata (has-ta-ta). L. "Hasta" (a spear). A second bot. name.

Hastate (has-tate). A botanical term used for a leaf whose lobes or ears at the bottom of the leaf stick out like the points of a halbert.

Hastilis (has-ti-lis). L. "Hastile" (the shaft of a spear). Second bot. name.

Hazel. Eng. name for Corylus group. Derived from A.S. "haesel," a baton of authority, because rods cut from it were used for driving slaves and cattle.

Heartsease. Eng. name for one of the Violets; gets this name because herbalists thought it a good cordial.

Heath. A.S. "Haeth." Eng. name for Erica group. The Sea-heath belongs to Frankenia group.

Heather. Scotch word for Heath.

Hedera (hed-er-a-). L. name for "Ivy." Bot. name of a group.

Hederaceæ (hed-er-a-she-e). L. adj., "ivy-like"; from shape of leaf. A second bot. name.

Hederafolia (hed-er-a-fol-i-a). L. adj., "hedera" (ivy); "folia" (leaves). Second bot. name.

Hedypnois (hed-ip-nois). G. name for some kind of Dandelion (the two G. words mean "sweet-

breathing "). Is by some used as first bot. name
for Lesser Hawkbit.

Helenium (hel-en-i-um). After Helen of Troy—the
flowers are said to have sprung from her tears.
Second bot. name Elecampane.

Heliocharis (hel-i-o-karis). See Eleocharis.

Helianthemum (hel-i-an-the-mum). G. "Heilios"
(the sun); "anthos" (flower). Bot. name for
Rochrose group.

Helioscopia (hel-i-o-skop-ia). G. "Heilios" (the
sun); "scopo" (watcher); because the flower
keeps turning to the sun. Second bot. name.

Helix (he-liks). L. word meaning ". wound round or
twisted." But also used as a name for Ivy.
Second bot. name for Common Ivy.

Hellebore (hel-le-bor). Eng. name for Helleborus.

Helleborine (hel-le-bor-in). Eng. name for Cephalanthera group, Orchid family. See Helleborus.

Helleborus (her-le-bor-us). G. "Elein" (to take
away); "bora" (food); because the root produces
vomiting. Bot. name for Hellebore group.

Helminth (hel-minth). Eng. name for Helminthia
group.

Helminthia (hel-min-thia). G. "Helminthion" a small
worm); from the shape of the fruit. Bot. name
for Helminth group.

Helosciadium (hel-o-ski-ad-i-um). G. "Helos" (a
marsh); "sciadon" (an umbrella). Was the name
of a group now merged into that of Apium.

Hemistemon (hemi-stemon). G. "Hemi" (half);
"stemon" (upright). Second bot. name.

Hemlock. A.S. "Hoem" (a straw or haulm);
"leac" (a plant); from the many hollow stalks

the plant throws up. Eng. name for Conium
group. The Water Hemlock belongs to the Cowbane group.

Hemp. A.S. " Henep " (name of the plant).

Henbane. Has nothing to do with a poison for hens.
It is a corruption of its A.S. name " henne-belle,"
i.e., hanging bell, referring to the fruit hanging
down like a bell. Eng. name for Hyoscyamus
group.

Henbit. Eng. name for one of the Dead Nettles.

Heracleum (her-ak-le-um). After Hercules, who is said
to be the first to discover the plant was good for
pigs. Bot. name for Hogweed group.

Herb. A common affix to many names of plants. Each
plant is given under its own letter—Herb Bennet,
under B (Bennet); Herb Christopher, under C
(Christopher); and so on.

Herbacea (her-ba-she-a). L. adj., " herb-like "; from
the size of the plant.

Herminium (her-min-i-um). G. word for the foot of a
bed; from the shape of the root. Bot. name Musk
group, Orchid family.

Herniaria (her-ne-ar-ia). L. " Hernia " (a rupture);
the plant used as a remedy for. Bot. name for
Rupture group.

Hesperis (hes-per-is). G. for " evening," the time
when the flower gives out its scent. Bot. name
for a group.

Heterophyllus (het-er-o-fil-lus). G. " Hetero " (different); " phyllus " (leaf); applied to many
different plants whose leaves are not all of one
shape. A second bot. name.

Heyneana. Second bot. name for a variety Bitter Cress.

Hexander (heks-an-der). G. "Hex" (six); "andros" (males); *i.e.*, six-stamened. Second bot. name.

Hiberna (hi-ber-na).

Hibernica (hi-ber-ne-ka). L. name for Ireland. Second bot. name.

Hieracium (hi-er-ak-i-um). G. "Hierakion" (name of a salve used by the Greeks for strengthening the eye-sight, in which Hawks' (G. "hieraka") eyes were probably used. Bot. name for Hawk-weed group (which see).

Hieracoides (hi-er-ak-oi-des). G. "Hieracium" (which see); "oides" (like). A second bot. name.

Hierochloe (hi-er-o-klo-e). G. "Hieros" (sacred); "chloe" (grass). Bot. name for Holy-Grass group. In olden times this was the grass used for strewing in the churches.

Hippocrepis (hip-po-cre-pis). G. "Hippo" (a horse); "crepis" (a shoe); from the shape of the pods. Bot. name for a group.

Hippophae (hip-po-fa-e). G. "Hippo" seems to be a mistake for "hypo" (under); "phaino" (to show light); the underside of leaf being very silvery. Bot. name for a group.

Hippuris (hip-pu-ris). G. "Hippos" (a horse); "oura" (a tail). Bot. name for a group Mares-tail family. These plants, although like in looks, are not related to Horsetails. See Equisetum.

Hircina (hir-ke-na). L., adj., "smells like a goat." Second bot. name.

Hirculus (hir-cul-us). L. "A little goat." A second bot. name.

Hirsutus (hir-sut-us). L. adj., "rough or shaggy"; usually rendered "hairy." Second bot. name used for many plants.

Hirtus (hir-tus). L. adj., "rough." Second bot. name.

Hirtifolius (hir-ti-fol-i-us). L. "Hirtus" (rough); "folius" (leaf); *i.e.*, rough-leaved. Second bot. name.

Hirtiæformis (hir-ti-e-for-mis). L. "Hirtus" (rough); "formis" (shape). Second bot. name.

Hispid (his-pid). A bot. term when the hairs are many and stiff; "hirsute" is used when the hairs are dense but *not* stiff.

Hispidus (his-pid-us). L. adj., "shaggy." Second bot. name.

Holcus (hol-kus). L. name for some kind of Grass, but now used as bot. name for a group.

Holly. A.S. "Holegn." Is the Eng. name for Ilex group. The Sea-Holly belongs to Eringyum group.

Hollyhock. Has nothing to do with the Holly. By one of the freaks of spelling, it has an "l" too many. It ought to be Holy Hock, an old name for the Mallow.

Holmense (hol-men-se). G. "Oulomenos" (powerful). A second bot. name for Sand Leek.

Holoschoenus (hol-os-ko-en-us). G. name for some coarse rush used in making wicker work. Now used as a second bot. name.

Holosericea (holo-ser-ik-e). G. "Olos" (all); "serikos" (silk); from the silk-like look of the flower. Second bot. name.

Holosteum (holo-ste-um). G. "Olos" (all); "steon"

(bone). Was the name for some Greek plant, but now used as bot. name for a group; and also as a second bot. name.

Holosteumoides (holo-ste-um-oi-des). G. "Holosteum"; "oides" (like). A second bot. name.

Holy Grass. Eng. translation of Heirochloe (which see).

Homophyllus (homo-fil-lus). G. "Omos" (same); "phyllus" (leaf); i.e., all the leaves alike. Second bot. name.

Honchenya. After German botanist Honcheny, who died 1805. A synonym used by some for Arenaria.

Honewort. One of the Eng. names for Common Trinia.

Honeysuckle. Eng. name for the Honeydew found on the leaves of Lonicera group, Honeysuckle family.

Hookeri. After Hooker, the botanist. Second bot. name for a variety Narrow Smallreed, found only at Lough Neagh, Ireland.

Hop. L. "Hupa" (hop plant). Bot. name for Humulus group.

Horedeum (hor-de-um). L. name for Barley. Bot. name for group Grass family.

Hordeaceus (hor-de-a-she-us). L. "Hordeum"; "aceous" (like); i.e., Barley-like. A second bot. name.

Horehound. Eng. name for Marrubium group. "Hore" is a corruption of A.S. "har" (grey), from the grey-like woolly down on the stems; "hound" has nothing to do with the dog; it is a corruption of A.S. "hune" (a strong smell), which the plant has. Besides this one, there is another Horehound; belonging to Ballota group, having also a strong disagreeable smell. The first is distinguished as White, the second as Black Horehound.

Horridus (hor-rid-us). L. adj., "rough or prickly." Second bot. name.

Hornbeam. Eng. name for Carpinus group (which see).

Horned Pondweed. Eng. name for Zannichellia group; called "horned" because of the look of the fruit, and to distinguish these plants from the common Pondweed.

Hornwort. Eng. translation of its bot. name Ceratophyllum (which see).

Horsetail. Common Eng. name for plants of Equisetum group.

Hortensis (hor-ten-sis). L. "Hortus" (a garden); i.e., belonging to the garden. A second bot. name.

Hottonia. After Hotton, botanist, died 1709. Bot. name of group.

Hounds' Tongue. Eng. translation of bot. name Cynoglossum group.

House Leek. Eng. name for Sempervivum group; and so called because the plant is often found growing on the roof of houses.

Humilis (hu-mil-is). L. adj., "on the ground." A second bot. name.

Humulus (hu-mul-us). L. "Humus" (ground or mould). Bot. name for Hop group.

Huma-fusa (hu-ma-fu-sa). L. "Humus" (ground); "fusa" (spread). A second bot. name for some plants that spread over the ground.

Hutchinsia. After Miss Hutchins, an Irish botanist,

9

and the only woman so honoured. Bot. name for group.

Hyacinth. Eng. name.

Hyacinthus (hi-a-sinth-us). G. name of a boy accidentally killed by Apollo, and from whose blood the flowers were created. First bot. name for the Bluebell, before, that flower was in the Squill group.

Hybridum (hi-brid-um). L. adj., " a cross between two plants, an mongrel." A rather common second bot. name.

Hydrocharis (hi-dro-kar-is). G. " Hydro " (water); " charis " (graceful); i.e., graceful water plants. Bot. name for Frogbit group.

Hydrocharideæ. G. "Hydrocharis"; "idaea" (like). Bot. name of family.

Hydrocotyle (hi-dro-ko-ti-le). " Hydro " (water); " kotule " (a cup); from the shape of the leaf. Bot. name Pennywort group.

Hydrolapathum (hi-dro-la-pa-thum). G. " Hydro " (water); " lapathum " (sorrel). Second bot. name for Water Dock.

Hydropiper (hi-dro-pi-per). G. " Hydro " (water); " peperi " (pepper). Second bot. name.

Hymale (hi-ma-le). L. " Hiems " (the winter time). Second bot. name.

Hymenophyllum (hi-men-o-fil-lum). G. " Hymen " (a membrane); " phyllon " (a leaf). Bot. name Filmy Fern group.

Hyoscyamus (hi-o-si-a-mus). G. " Hus " (a hog); " kuamos " (a bean). Bot. name Henbane group.

Hyperborea (hi-per-bo-re-a). G. " Uper " (beyond); " boreas " (the North wind); i.e., Northern.

Hypericum (hi-per-i-kum). G. name for St. John's

-wort plant. Bot. name for a group, and Eng.
name for family. This plant is said to be a great
charm against evil spirits.

Hypericineæ (hi-per-i-se-ne-e). Bot. name for Hypericum family.

Hypochœre (hi-po-ko-er-e). Eng. rendering of Hypo-
choeris, a group of Composite family.

Hypochœris (hi-po-ko-er-is). G. "Hypo" (for);
"choeris" (the hog); because pigs eat the roots.
Bot. name for a group.

Hypochœroides (hi-po-ko-er-oi-des). G. "Hypo-
choeris" and "oides" (like). Second bot. name.

Hypnoides (hip-noi-des). G. "Uphon" (moss);
"oides" (like). Second bot. name.

Hypopithys (hi-po-pith-is). G. "Hypo" (under);
"pitus" (a fir tree); where the plant is usually
found. Second bot. name.

Hyssop (his-sup). L. "Hyssopus"; name of a well-
known plant.

Hyssopifolium (his-sup-i-fol-i-um). L. "Hyssop" and
"folium" (a leaf); hyssop-leaved. A second bot.
name.

Hystrix (his-triks). G. "Hystrix" (a porcupine);
from the number of jagged brown scales with which
the root stock is covered. Second bot. name for
a variety, found in Guernsey, of Isoetes-Quillwort.

I

Iberis (i-be-ris). After an old L. name for Spain, where
the plant is very common. Bot. name for Candytuft.

Idæus (i-da-us). After Mount Ida, Crete, where the

Raspberry grows abundantly. A second bot. name.

Illecebraceæ (il-le-se-bra-se-e). L. " Illecebrum " and "aceous " (like). Bot. name for a family.

Illecebrum (il-le-se-brum). Means in L. "attraction," but was also name for some plant. Now bot. name of a group.

Illyricus (il-le-ri-kus). L. name for country N.E. side of Adriatic. Now belongs to Austria. Second bot. name.

Ilvensis (il-ven-sis). Second bot. name for Alpine Woodsia.

Imbricatus (im-bre-ka-tus). L. "Arranged after the manner of tiles," one overlapping the other." A second bot. name.

Impatiens (im-pa-she-ens). L. adj., " hasty," because when ripe the pods with the slightest touch fly open and scatter its seeds." Bot. name Balsam group.

Implexa (im-pleks-a). L. adj., "entwining." A second bot. group.

Incana (in-ka-na). L. adj., " quite grey, hoary." Second bot. name.

Incarnata (in-kar-na-ta). L. adj., " clothed in flesh "; i.e., flesh-coloured. Second bot. name.

Incisum (in-si-sum). L. adj., " cut into "; the upper leaves are deeply cut into. Second bot. name.

Incubacea (in-ku-ba-se-a). L. " Incubo " (to lie down); from a characteristic of the plant. A second bot. name.

Incumbens (in-kum-bens). L. adj., "leaning on." Second bot. name.

Incurva (in-kur-va). L. adj., " bent " (the stem often bent or curved. A second bot. name.

Incurvifolia (in-kur-ve-fol-ia). L. adj., "curved leaf." A second bot. name.

Inermis (in-erm-is). L. adj., "unarmed"; because it has no spines. Second bot. name.

Infesta (in-fes-ta). L. adj., "troublesome." A second bot. name.

Inflata (in-fla-ta). L. adj., "puffed out"; from the inflated pod. Second bot. name.

Innata (in-na-ta). L. adj., "inborn." A second bot. name.

Inodora (in-o-do-ra). L. adj., "no smell." Second bot. name.

Institia (in-sti-te-a). L. adj., "grafted." Second bot. name for a variety of Blackthorn; the original of all the Plums.

Intacta (in-tak-ta). L. adj., "entire"; from the tubers being entire. Second bot. name.

Integrifolia (in-te-gri-fol-ia). L. "Integer" (whole); "folia" (leaves). Second bot. name.

Intermedia (in-ter-med-ia). L. adj., "halfway." Second bot. name.

Intybus (in-te-bus). Was G. name for Chicory, but is now used as its second bot. name.

Inula (in-u-la). G. diminutive of Helen (of Troy). Is bot. name Inule group.

Inuloides (in-u-loi-des). G. "Inula"; "oides." (like). Second bot. name.

Inundatum (in-un-da-tum). L. adj., "overflowed"; *i.e.*, sometimes wet, sometimes dry; where the plant like growing. Second bot. name.

Involuta (in-vo-lu-ta). L. adj., "edges of the leaf turned in." Second bot. name.

Iricum (ir-ik-um). L. "Hiricus" (smell of a goat). Second bot. name.

Irio (i-ri-o). Was the L. name of the plant which the G. called ".Erysimum." Now used as second bot. name for the London Rocket.

Irideæ (i-ri-de-e). Bot. name for the Iris family.

Iris (i-ris). G. name for the Rainbow; the name is given because the flowers are of so many different colours. Bot. name for both a family and a group.

Irrigua (ir-rig-u-a). L. adj., "swampy"; where the plant grows. Second bot. name.

Isatis (is-a-tis). G. name for Woad. Bot. name for Woad group.

Isnardia (is-nard-ia). After the French botanist Isnard, who died 1743. Used as bot. name for a group by Linneus for what is now Ludwigia.

Isoetes (i-so-e-tes). G. "Iso" (the same); "etos" (a year); *i.e.*, evergreen. Bot. name Quillwort group.

Isolepis (i-so-le-pes). G. "Iso" (equal); "lepes" (scales); refers to the size of the scales on the flowers. Is the bot. group name of some botanists for Scripus group.

Italicum (it-al-i-kum). "Italian" in Latin dress. Second bot. name for Italian Rye-grass.

J

Jacob's Ladder. Eng. name for Polemonium Caeruleum. Said to be so called from the ladder-like look the leaves have of growing.

Jacobæa (jak-o-be-a). L. for James. Second bot. name for Ragwort, which is also called St. James' Wort.

Jasione (jas-i-on-e). G. name of some similar plant. Now bot. name for a group.

Jasminaceæ (jas-min-a-se-e).- Was the bot. name in the first edition of Bentham and Hooker " British Flora " for Olive family.

Jasmine or Jessamine. Eng. name for Jasminum.

Jasminum (jas-min-um). Arabic. - " Yasmin " (name of the plant).

Juncaceæ (jung-a-se-e). L. "Juncus " and " aceous " (like). Bot. name Rush family.

Jungus (jung-kus). L. " Jungo " (to bind); because the plants were used for tying up things. Bot. name for Rush group.

Junceum (jung-se-um). L. adj., " made of rushes." Second bot. name.

Juncifolia (jung-se-fol-ia). L. adj., " rush-leaved "; the leaves of the plant being like the rush. A second bot. name.

Juranum. Second bot. synonym for Prenanth Hawkweed.

Juniperus (jew-ne-per-us). L. name of plant. Bot. name for Juniper group.

Jerusalem-Artichoke. " Jerusalem " is a corruption of Italian " girasole," a flower that turns towards the sun.

K

Kale or Kail. A.S. " Cawl," the common name for one of the cultivated cabbages—Brassica oleracea.

Kidney Vetch. Called " kidney " because the plant was in the days of old thought good for diseases of that organ.

Knappia. After Knapp, an Eng. botanist, who died 1845. Name given by some botanists to group Mibroa.

Knapweed. A corruption of Knopweed, from the knob-like look of the head. Eng. name for a group.

Knautia (nawt-ia). After Knaut, a Saxony botanist, died 1716. Bot. name used by some botanists as the group name of Field Scabious.

Knawel (naw-el). Eng. name for Scleranthus group.

Knotgrass.

Knotweed. Does not belong to the Grass family. Eng. name for Polygonum family. Gets name "Grass" from knottiness of its stem, and is freely eaten by cattle.

Kobresia (kob-res-ia). After Kobres, of Augsberg, a patron of botany. Bot. name for a group.

Kœleria (koel-er-ia). After Koeler, a German botanist, who died 1807. Bot. name for a group.

Kœniga (ko-nig-a). After Mr. Konig, of British Museum. Is the group name used by some, instead of Alyssum, for Sweet Alyssim.

Kraka (kra-ka). Norse name for "crow," whence probably by translation we get the "crow" in Crowberry.

Kohlrabbi (kol-rub-be). German. "Kohl-rube" (kale-turnip); a cultivated variety of Kale or Cabbage.

L

Labiate (la-be-ate). L. "Labium" (a lip); from the flowers of this family having their petals more or less like the upper and lower lips of a mouth. Bot. name a large family, containing 18 groups.

Lachenalii. After Lachenal. Second bot. name Parsley Œnanth.

Laciniata (la-sin-e-ata). L. "Lacinia" (the flap of a garment); *i.e.*, narrow-lobed. A second bot. name.

Lactea (lak-te-a). L. adj., "milky-white." Second bot. name.

Lactuca (la-tu-ka). L. adj., "full of milk"; from the milky juice of the stem. Bot. name for Lettuce group.

Lacustris (la-kus-tris). L. "Lacus" (a pond); where the plant grows. Second bot. name.

Ladanum (lad-a-num). G. "Ledon" (name of shrub whence resin was got). Second bot. name for Red Galeopsis.

Lady's. When this word forms part of a plant's name it may be assumed that it refers to "Our Lady"— the Virgin Mary. In days of old monks and nuns were fond of dedicating all sorts of flowers to her. But how the second part of the name applies is not always clear.

Ladies' Bedstraw. Eng. name for Galium verum; gets this name from its soft puffy stems having, in former days, been used, even by ladies of rank, to sleep upon. The phrase "being in straw," when a woman is confined, is said to come from straw being laid down in front of the house to deaden the noises.

Lady Fern. A translation of second bot. name of plant.

Lady's-Fingers. One of the Eng. names for Anthyllis Vulneraria; from its soft inflated calyx.

Lady's Mantle. Eng. name for Alchemillia Vulgaris; from the shape and vandyked edge of the leaf.

Lady's Slipper. Translation of first bot. name of the flower, " Lady " taking the place of " Venus."

Lady's Smock. One of the Eng. names for Cardamine Pratensis. Said to be from the shape of the flower, which are thought to be like little smocks laid out on the meadow to dry.

Lady's Tresses. Eng. name for Spiranthes group; from the flowers on the spike being like braided hair.

Laete-Virens (la-te-vi-rens). L. " Laete " (pleasant); " virens " (green). Second bot. name.

Lævigata (la-vi-ga-ta). L. adj., " smooth." Second bot. name.

Lævis (la-vis). L. adj., " polished, smooth." A second bot. name.

Lagopina (lag-o-pi-na). G. " Lago " (a hare); " pous " (a foot); from the plant having long hairs, like those of a hare's foot. Second bot. name for Hare's Foot Carex.

Lagurus (lag-u-rus). G. " Lago " (a hare); " urus " (a tail). Bot. name for the Hare's-Tail group.

Lamb's Lettuce. One of the Eng. names for Valerianella Olitoria; because the plant appears at the lambing season.

Lamb's Succory. One of the Eng. names for Arnoseris Pusilla.

Lamium (la-mi-um). G. " Laimos " (the throat); from the throat-like look of the flowers. Bot. name for Dead Nettle group.

Lamottei. After La Motte. A second bot. name.

Lamprocarpus (lam-pro-car-pus). G. " Lamporos " (bright); " carpua " (fruit). Second bot. name.

Lamyi. After Lamy. A second bot. name.

Lanata (la-na-ta). L. adj., "woolly." Second bot. name.

Lancasteriense (lan-cas-ter-i-en-se). L. for " of Lancaster," because the plant was first found in Isle of Walney, Lancashire. Second bot. name.

Lanceolatum (lan-se-o-la-tum). L. adj., " small-lanced shape "; from the shape of the leaf. Second bot. name.

Lancefolia (lan-se-fol-ia). L. " Lancea " (a lance); " folia " (leaves); from the shape of the leaf. Second bot. name.

Lappa (lap-pa). L. for " a bur." Second bot. name for Burdock.

Lappacea (lap-pa-se-a).

Lapponica (lap-pon-i-ka).

Lapponum (lap-po-num). All three from L. " lappa " (a bur); adj., with different shade of meaning. Used as second bot. name.

Lantana (lan-ta-na). Italian name for the tree. Second bot. name Wayfaring tree.

Lapathifolium (lap-a-thi-fol-ium).—L. " Lapathum " (the dock); " folium " (leaf), i.e., dock-like leaf. Second bot. name.

Lapsana (lap-sa-na). G. name for some potable herb. A second bot. name.

Larch. Corruption of G. and L. name " Larix." One of Pine group.

Larkspur. Eng. name for Delphinium group; from the " spur," of the flower being long.

Lasiophyllum (las-i-o-fil-lum). G. " Lasios " (shaggy); " phyllum " (a leaf). A second bot. name.

Lastrea (las-tre-a). After De Lastre, a French botanist. Is a group name used by some botanists for Shield Fern.

Lathyris (la-thir-is). G. name for plant. Second bot. name Caper Spurge.

Lathyrus (la-thyr-us). G. name for that kind of Vetch. Bot. name Pea group.

Lathyroides (la-thir-oi-des). G. " Lathyrus "; "oides" (like). Second bot. name.

Latifolia (lat-i-fol-ia). L. " Latus " (broad); " folia " (leaves). A very common second bot. name for many plants of different groups and families.

Laurel (law-rel). L. name for the plant. The Laurel of the ancients, from which wreaths for victors were made, is what we call the Bay-tree— " Bay," from French " baie " (a berry). Our Laurel belongs now to Prunus group.

Laureola (law-re-o-la). L. diminutive of " Laurus."

Laurina (law-ri-na). L. " Laurel-like." Both are L. adj. Used as second bot. names.

Lavatera (lav-a-ter-a). After the two Lavaters, who were friends of the botanist Tournefort. Bot. name for a group.

Lavender (lav-en-der). L. " Lavendula " (name of the plant; from the verb " to wash "; because the ancients used it largely in their baths. Eng. name for a well-known cultivated plant. As Sea Lavender it is the name of Statice Limonium.

Laxa (laks-a). L. adj., " loose." Second bot. name.

Laxiflora (laks-i-flo-ra). L. " Laxus " (loose); " flora " (flowered). Second bot. name of the Loose Orchis.

Leadwort. Translation of L. name Plumbago.

Lecoqii. After Lecoq. Second bot. name for a variety of the Long-headed Poppy, whose sap, instead of white, is yellow.

Leek. A.S. " Leac " (name of the plant). The

garden Leek is a cultivated variety of the Wild Leek. It is the emblem of the Welsh, because green and white were the old Cymric colours, and these two colours are found combined in the Leek.

Leersia. After Leers, a German botanist, died 1774. Bot. name for a group.

Leguminosæ (legu-min-ose). L. "Legumen" (pulse). Bot. term applied to plants of the Bean or Pea kind.

Lemna (lem-na). G. "Lemna (a scale). Bot. name for Duckweed group.

Lemnaceæ (lemna-see-e). L. "Lemna" and "aceous" (like). Bot. name for the Duckweed family.

Lendigerum (len-di-je-rum). L. "Lens" (a nit); "gerum" (a carrier). Second bot. name Nitgrass.

Lenormandi. After Le Normand. A second bot. name.

Lentibulaceæ (len-ti-bul-a-se-e). L. "Lens" (lentil); "bula (a boss); "aceous" (like). Bot. name for Pinguicula family.

Lent Lily. "Lent" (a corruption of A.S. "lencten," Spring), which was so called because the days begin to lengthen. Eng. name for Daffodil, because that flower comes into bloom at that time.

Lentiginosus (len-tij-in-o-sus). L. adj., "full of freckles"; *i.e.*, minutely dotted over. A second bot. name.

Leontodon (le-on-to-don). G. "Leon" (a lion); "odous" (a tooth); from the tooth-like margins of the leaf. Bot. name for Hawkbit group.

Leonurus (le-on-ur-us). G. "Leon" (a lion); "ourus" (a tail); from some supposed resemblance of the plant. Bot. name for a group.

Leopard's Bane. Eng. name for Doronicum Parda-

lianches; so called because in days of old it was
mixed with flesh to destroy leopards.

Lepidium (lep-id-i-um). G. "Lepis" (a scale); from
the shape of the seed vessels. Bot. name Cress
group.

Lepidocarpa (lep-id-o-car-pa). G. "Lepis" (a scale);
"carpus" (a fruit). Second bot. name.

Lepigonum (lep-i-go-num). G. "Lepis" (a scale);
"gonum" (a joint). A synonym for Sandspurry
group.

Leporina (lep-or-ina). G. "Lepus" (a hare). A
second bot. name.

Leptoclados (lep-to-cla-dos). G. "Leptos" (thin);
"clados" (branched). Second bot. name.

Leptophyllia (lep-to-fil-lia). G. "Leptos" (thin);
"phullon" (leaved). A second bot. name.

Lepturus (lep-tu-rus). G. "Leptos" (thin); "ourus"
(tail); from the curved tail-like look of the spike.
Bot. name of a group.

Lettuce (let-tus) Eng. rendering of "Lactuca." The
bot. name for group.

Leucanthemum (lu-can-the-mum). G. "Leukos"
(white); "anthos" (flower). A second bot. name.

Leucochroa (lu-ko-kro-a). G. "Leukos" (white);
"chroas" (surface); i.e., white-coloured. Second
bot. name.

Leucoium (lu-ko-ium). G. "Leukos" (white); "ion"
(violet). Bot. name Snowflake group.

Leucostachys (lu-ko-sta-chis). G. "Leukos" (white);
"stachus" (ear). Second bot. name.

Libanotis (lib-an-o-tis). G. name for the gum got from
a tree, "Libanos." Second bot. name.

Lichen (litsh-en). G. "Leichen." (name of the plant);

sometimes called Tree or Rock Moss, because these fungus-like plants are found growing there.

Ligulatae (lig-u-late). L. " Ligula " (a little tongue); applied to the petals of Dandelion and Hawkweed, from their tongue or strap-like shape.

Ligerica (lig-er-i-ka). After Liguria, the old name of a part of North Italy. A second bot. name.

Lignosa (lig-no-sa). L. adj., " woody." A second bot. name.

Ligusticum (lig-ust-i-kum). After Liguria, where the plants grows abundantly. Bot. name for Lovage group.

Ligustrum (lig-us-trum). L. name for Privet. Bot. name for Privet group.

Liliaceæ (lil-e-a-she-e). L. " Lilium " (a lily). and " aceous " (like). Bot. name for Lily family.

Lily of the Valley. " Of the valley " is but a translation of the L. " convallaria," the name of the group.

Lime. Corruption of its old name Linde, which meant " pliant," referring to its bast. Eng. name Tilia group.

Limnanth (lim-nanth). Eng. name for Limnanthemum group.

Limnanthemum (lim-nanth-e-mum). G. " Limne " (a marsh); " anthos " (a flower). Bot. name for Limnanth group.

Limonium (lim-on-i-um). G. " Limonios " (a meadow). Second bot. name.

Limosel (lim-o-sel). Eng. name for Limosella group.

Limosella (lim-o-sel-la). L. " Limus " (mud); where the plant grows. Bot. name for a group.

Limosum (lim-o-sum). L. adj., "muddy." Second bot. name.

Linaceæ (lin-a-se-e). L. "Linum" (flax); "aceous." (like). Bot. name Flax family.

Linum (li-num). L. "Linum" (flax). Bot. name for a group.

Linaria (li-nar-ia). L. "Linum" (flax); the leaves of plants of this group being like those of the Flax. Bot. name for a group.

Linarifolium (li-nar-i-fol-i-um). L. "Linari" (flax-like); "folium" (leaf). A second bot. name.

Ling. A.S. "Lig" (fuel). Eng. name for Calluna group.

Lingulatum (ling-u-la-tum). L. adj., "tongue-shaped." A second bot. name.

Linnaea (lin-a-e-a). After Linneus, the great botanist, with whom this flower was a favourite. Bot. name group.

Linosyris (lin-o-ser-is). A term used by Pliny for plant with leaves and branches like those of the Flax. Second bot. name.

Linophyllum (lin-o-fil-lum). G. "Lino" (flax); "phyllum" (leaf); i.e., flax-like-leaf. Second bot. name.

Linseed (lin-seed). A.S. "Lin-saed" (seed of the Flax).

Linum (li-num). G. name for Flax. Bot. name for Flax group.

Liparis (lip-ar-is). G. "liparos" (fatty); from the unctious feel of the leaf. Bot. name for a group.

Listera (lis-ter-a). After Lister, English botanist, died 1711. Bot. name Twayblade group.

Lithosperum (lith-o-sper-mum). G. "Lithos" (a

stone); "sperma" (seed); from the hardness of the seed. Bot. name Gromwell group.

Lithuanicus (lith-u-an-i-kus). L. adj., "suffering from the stone"; probably used as a remedy for the disease. Second bot. name.

Littorel (lit-to-rel). Eng. rendering of "Littorella" (which see).

Littorella (lit-tor-el-la). L. adj., "belonging to the sea-shore." Bot. name for a group.

Littoralis (lit-tor-alis). L. adj., "belonging to the sea-shore." A common second bot. name for many plants.

Lividus (liv-i-dus). L. adj., "bluish-black." A second bot. name.

Livelong. Tells is own derivation; another name for Orpine.

Lizard Orchis. Gets its name "Lizard" from the sup-posed resemblance of flower to a Lizard.

Lloydia (loyd-i-a). After Lyod, a Welsh botanist, who first discovered the plant in Britain. Bot. name for a group.

Lobatum (lo-ba-tum). G. "Lobos" (lower part of the ear). Second bot. name.

Lobelia (lo-be-le-a). After Lobel, botanist, died 1616. Bot. name group.

Lobularis (lo-bu-lar-is). L. adj., "having a little lobe." Second bot. name.

Locusta (lo-kus-ta). L. for "locust." A second bot. name.

Loeselii. After Loesel. Second bot. name for Two-leaved Liparis.

Loiseleuria. After Loiseleur, French botanist, died 1849. Bot. name for group.

Lolium (lo-li-um). L. name for "darnel." Bot. name for a group.

Loliacea (lo-li-a-se-e).. L. adj., "lolium"; "aceous" (like). Second bot. name.

Lomaria (lom-ar-ia). G. "Loma" (a fringe); from the row of seeds on the back of leaf. The group name of some botanists for Blechnum.

Lonchitis (lon-ki-tis).. G. adj., "spear-like." A second bot. name.

Lonchitidoides (lon-ki-ti-doi-des). G. "Lonchitis"; "oides" (like). A second bot. name.

London Pride. Eng. name for Saxifraga umbrosa. Gets its name "London" from a Mr. London, of the firm London and Wise, Royal Gardeners, who introduced the plant early in the 18th Century. See St. Patrick's Cabbage.

London Rocket. Eng. name for Sisymbrium Irio. Gets its name London from the fact that after the fire of 1666, a large crop suddenly sprung up in and about London. See Rocket.

Loose Strife. A translation of the group name "Lysimachia." There are two Loose Strifes—one belonging to Lysimachia group; the other to Lythrum group; quite different plants.

Loranthaceæ (lor-an-tha-se-e). G. "Loron" (a thong); from the leathery, thong-like look of the leaf; "anthus" (a flower); "aceous" (like). Bot. name Mistletoe family.

Lords and Ladies. One of the many names of the Common Arum.

Loroglossum (lo-ro-glos-sum). G. "Loron" (a thong); "glossum" (tongue); from the shape of the petals. Group name of some botanists for Lizard Orchis.

Lotus (lo-tus). G. name for several plants. Now the
bot. name for a group of Peaflower family.

Louse Wort. Translation of bot. group name Pedicularis.

Lovage. Eng. name for Ligusticum group; before
called Loveache.

Lucern. Eng. name for Medicago sativa, apparently
named after Lucerne in Switzerland.

Ludwigia. After Ludwig, Professor of Botany, died
1773. Bot. name for a group.

Lucens (lu-sens).

Lucidum (lu-si-dum). Both L. adj., " shining."
Second bot. names.

Lunaria (lun-ar-ia). L. adj., " belonging to the moon."
Second bot. name of Moon Wort.

Lung Wort. Translation of bot. group name Pulmonaria.

Lupulina (lu-pul-ina).

Lupulus (lu-pul-us). Both from L. " lupulus," (a wolf).
Second bot. names. Lupulus was the herbalists'
shop name for Hop.

Lusitanica (lus-i-tan-ik-a). From Lusitania, the name
of an old Roman province, in South of Spain.
Second bot. name Pale Butterwort. This plant
extends along the West coast of Europe from Spain
to Scotland.

Lutea (lu-te-a). L. adj., " yellow." A common second
bot. name.

Luteo-Album (lu-te-o-al-bum). L. adj., " yellowish
white." A second bot. name.

Luteola (lu-te-o-la). L. adj., " yellowish." Second
bot. name.

Lutescens (lu-tes-sens). L. adj., " becoming yellow."
Second bot. name.

Lutetiana (lu-te-shi-a-na). L. adj., " yellowish."
Second bot. name.

Luteo-Virescens (lu-te-o-vi-res-sens). L. " Lutus "
(yellow); " virescens " (turning green). A second
bot. name.

Luzula (lu-zu-la). Italian. " Luzulae " (a glow worm);
which comes from L. " luceo " (to shine); the pith
of the plant was used for the wicks of lamps. Bot.
name Woodrush group.

Lychnis (lik-nis). G. " Luchnis " (giving light); from
the down being used as wicks for lamps. Bot.
name for group.

Lychnites (lik-ni-tes). G. " Luchnis " (giving light).
A second bot. name.

Lycopodiaceæ (li-ko-po-de-a-se-e). G. " Lycopodium "
and " aceous " (like). Bot. name for Clubmoss
family.

Lycopodium (li-ko-po-di-um). G. " Lukos " (a wolf);
" pous " (a foot); from the footlike look of the
branches. Bot. name for group.

Lycopsis (li-kop-sis). G. " Lukos " (a wolf); " opsis "
(figure); the flower supposed to be like a wolf. Bot.
name Bugloss group.

Lycopus (li-ko-pus). G. " Lukos " (a wolf); " pous "
(a foot); from the shape of the leaf. Bot. name for
a group.

Lymegrass. Eng. name for Elymus group.

Lynosiris. See Linosyris.

Lysimachia (le-sim-a-kia). G. " Lusis " (freeing
from); " machios " (strife). Pliny tells us that it
was so named because if the plant is put about their

yokes when ploughing, the oxen will not fight; but others say it was called after Lysimuchus, King of Macedon, the first to find out the goodness of the plant. Bot. name for Primrose group.

Lythrareæ (lith-ra-re-e). Bot. name for Lythrum family.

Lythrum (lith-rum). G. word for "blood"; from the colour of the flowers. Bot. name for a group.

M

Macrocephalum (mak-ro-se-fal-um). G. "Makros" (long); "cephale" (head). Second bot. name.

Macorphyllum (mak-ro-fil-lum). G. "Makros" (long); "phullon" (leaf). Second bot. name.

Macrorhizus (mak-ro-riz-us). G. "Makros" (long); "riza" (a root). Second bot. name.

Macrostemon (mak-ro-ste-mon). G. "Makros" (long); "stemon" (stamen). Second bot. name.

Maculatus (mak-u-la-tus). L. "Macula" (a spot); *i.e.*, spotted. A common second bot. name for many different plants.

Madder. A.S. "Maeddere." Eng. name for Rubia group. The root of the plant is used for dying red.

Madritensis. A second bot. name.

Maianthemum (ma-i-an-the-mum). G. "Mai" (mother of Mercury, to whom the month of May was dedicated); "anthemum" (a flower). Bot. name for May Lily group.

Maidenhair. Translation of second bot. name, but "maiden" takes the place of "Venus." Eng. name for Adiantum group.

Majalis (ma-ja-lis). G. adj., "belonging to May." Second bot. name.

Major (ma-jur).

Majus (ma-jus). L. "Magnus" (great). A common second bot. name applied to many different plants.

Malachium (mal-ak-i-um). G. "Malakos" (soft). A group name of botanists for Stellaria.

Malaxis (mal-ak-is). G. "Malaxos" (soft); from the nature of the ground where the plant grows. Bot. name for Bog Orchis group.

Male Fern. Translation of plant's second bot. name.

Mallow (mal-low). G. "Malaxos" (soft); so called from its softening properties on the phlegm of colds. Its flat fruits are called cheeses by children. Eng. name for Malva group.

Multi-Florus (mul-ti-flo-rus). L. adj., "many flowered." Second bot. name.

Malva (mal-va). L. name for Mallow; from the soft downy leaves of the plant. Bot. name for Mallow group.

Malvaceæ (mal-va-se-e). L. "Malva" and "aceous" (like). Bot. name for Mallow family.

Man Orchis. Translation of the plant's second bot. name, which was given because the flower is like the figure of a man as drawn by children.

Mangel-Wurzel (mang-gl-wur-zel). German "mangel" (scarcity); "wurzel" (root); is a cultivated variety of the Wild-Beet.

Maple. Celtic. "Mapwl" (name of tree from its knotty excrescences). Eng. name for Acer group.

Malus (ma-lus). L. "Malum" (an apple). Second bot. name Crab-apple.

Maram (mar-am). Danish. " Marhalm " (sea-haulm). Eng. name Psamma group.

Marestail. Translation of G. group name Hippuris. Marestail, although like in look, are not allied to Horsetail.

Marigold. " Mari " (after Virgin Mary); gold " (from the colour of the flower).

Margaritacea (mar-ga-rit-a-se-e). L. " Margarita " (a pearl); " aceous " (like). A second bot. name.

Marginata (mar-jin-a-ta). L. adj., " having a border "; *i.e.*, broad-brimmed. A second bot. name.

Marianus (ma-ri-a-nus). " Mary " in Latin dress; refers to Virgin Mary, whose milk, it is said, falling on the leaves of a Thistle, caused its white, milk-like veins. A second bot. name.

Marinum (ma-reen-um). L. adj., " marine." A second bot. name.

Marifolium (mar-i-fol-i-um). L. " Mari " (the sea); " folium " (leaf). A second bot. name first used for Hoary Rockrose.

Mariscus (mar-is-kus). L. name for some kind of fig. A second bot. name.

Marjoram (ma-jo-ram). Said to be a corruption of its G. name " amarakos." Eng. name for Origanum group.

Maritimus (mar-e-tim-us). L. adj., " belonging to the sea." A very common second bot. name applied to many plants.

Marrubium (mar-rub-i-um). From the Hebrew name for one of the five bitter herbs ordered to be eaten by the Jews at the Feast of the Passover. Bot. name for a group.

Marsilea (mar-sil-ea). Eng. name for a family.

Marsilaceæ (mar-sil-a-se-e). L. " Marsil " and
" aceous " (like). Bot. name for a family.

Mascula (mas-ku-la). L. adj., " masculine." Second
bot. name Early Orchis.

Master Wort. Translation of its old L. name " Im-
peratoria." Eng. name for one of the Peucedans.

Matgrass. Eng. name for Nardus group. Gets its
" mat " from the dense tufted way it grows.

Matricaria (ma-trik-ar-ia). The old L. name for the
plant; from " matrix " (the womb), the plant being
used for diseases of. Bot. name for a group.

Matricary (ma-trik-a-re). Eng. name for above.

Matronalis (ma-tron-al-is). L. adj., " belonging to a
married woman "; hence the " Dame " in its Eng.
name. Second bot. name for Dame's Violet.

Matteiola (mat-te-o-la). After Mattioli, an Italian
botanist, died 1577. Bot. name Stock group.

Matweed. Eng. name for " Sea Matweed," for
plant Maram group. Gets " mat " from its dense
mat-like tufts.

May. Common Eng. name for the Hawthorn. Takes
it from the name of the month in which it blossoms.

May Lily. Eng. name for Maianthemum group.

May Weed. Eng. name for Matricaria Inodora. Stink
Mayweed is Eng. name for Anthemis Cotula.

May Wort. Eng. name for Crosswort-Galium Cruciata.
All the above three take " May " from the month
in which they flower.

Meadowsweet. Eng. name for one of the Spireas.
Gets its " sweet " from its many sweet-scented
flowers.

Meconopsis (me-kon-op-sis). G. " Mecon " (a poppy);
" opsis " (like). Bot. name for a group.

Media (me-de-a). L. adj.,.'' mid-way.'' A second bot.
name.

Medicago (med-ik-a-go). G. '' Medike '' (the name
given to a clover because it had been brought by
the Medes into Greece). Bot. name for a group.

Medick (med-ik). Eng. rendering of above.

Mediterranea (med-e-ter-ra-ne-a). L. adj., '' of the
Mediterranean.''

Medlar. A corruption of A.S. '' medle-tree.'' Is the
Eng. name for Mespilus group.

Megastachyum (meg-as-tak-ium). G. '' Megas ''
(great); '' stachus '' (an ear of corn). A second
bot. name.

Melampyrum (mel-am-pi-rum). G. '' Melas '' (black);
'' puros '' (wheat); from the seeds being in shape
like those of wheat. Bot. name for a group.

Melanocephalium (mel-an-o-se-fa-li-um). G. '' Melas ''
(black);'' cephale '' (head). Second bot. name.

Meleagris (mele-a-gris). G. name for the guinea-fowl.
Used as second bot. name for Common Fritillary,
because of the markings of the flower.

Melica (mel-i-ka). L. '' Mel '' (honey); from the sweet
taste of the stem.

Melick (mel-ick). Eng. rendering for above.

Melilot (mel-e-lot). Eng. rendering for below.

Melilotus (mel-i-lo-tus). L. '' Mel '' (honey); '' lotus.''
(which see). Bot. name for a group.

Melissophyllum (mel-is-so-fi-lum). G. '' Melissa '' (a
bee); '' phullon '' (a leaf). Second bot. name.

Melittis (mel-it-tis). G. Another form of '' melissa '' (a
bee). Bot. name for a group.

Membranacea (mem-bran-a-se-a). L. '' Membrane ''

(thin transparent tissue); " aceous " (like). Second bot. name.

Mentha (men-tha). G. name of a nymph whom Prosperine changed into the plant Mint. Bot. name for a group.

Menyanthes (men-e-an-thes). G. " Men " (a month); "anthos " (a flower); because the bloom was supposed to last for a month. Bot. name Buckbean group.

Menziesia (me-ne-se-a). After Menzies, a botanist, died 1842. Bot. name for a group.

Mercurialis (mer-cur-i-al-is). L. After the god Mercury. Bot. name for the Mercury group.

Mertensia (mer-ten-si-a). After Mertens, a German botanist, died 1831. Bot. name for a group.

Mespilus (mes-pi-lus). G. name for Medlar-tree. Bot. name Medlar group.

Meu. Looks like a contraction of Meum.

Meum (me-um). G. name for one of the Umbellate family. Now bot. name for Spignel group.

Mezereum (mes-er-e-um). One derivation is that the word is a Latinized form of Madzaryoun, the Persian name of the plant; another that it is a corruption of " Missir " (Egypt) and " oon " (a flower); *i.e.*, the Egyptian flower. Second bot. name of Mezereon, a plant of Daphne group. Its red berries are very poisonous.

Mibora (mi-bo-ra). Bot. name group of Grass family.

Micani (mi-ka-ni). L. adj., " quivering." Second bot. name.

Micranthus (mi-kran-thus). G. " Mikros " (small); "anthus " (flower). Second bot. name.

Microcala (mi-kro-ka-la). G. " Mikros " (small);

" kalon " (wood). First bot. name of some botanists for the Cicendia group.

Microcephalum (mi-kro-se-fa-lum). G. "Mikros" (small); "kephale " (a head). Second bot. name.

Microphyllum (mik-ro-fil-lum). G. "Mikros " (small); " phullon " (leaf). Second bot. name.

Microspermum (mik-ro-sper-mum). G. "Mikros " (small); " sperma " (a seed). Second.

Mid-Summer-Men. Another Eng. name for Roseroot, one of the Stonecrop group. It gets this name from an old English village custom. On Mid-summer Eve the girls each pulled up two plants, one for herself, the other for her " man." Placed side by side, the fidelity of the lovers was proved by the way the plants turned to or from each other.

Mielchoferi (mil-ko-fer-i). G. "Mielcho" (honey); L. " feri " (bearer). Second bot. name.

Mignonette (min-yo-net). French diminutive of " mignon " (darling). Eng. name for Reseda group and family.

Milfoil (mil-foyl). Eng. rendering of Millefolium (which see).

Milium (mil-e-um). L. " Millia " (thousands); from its many seeds. Bot. name for a group, Grass family.

Milkwort. Free translation of its bot. name " Poly-gala " (much milk); because the plant was sup-posed to increase the flow of milk. Eng. name for a group and family.

Millefolium (mil-fol-i-um). L. " Millia " (thousands); " folia " (leaves); because of the many leaflets into which the leaf is divided. A second bot. name.

Millegrana (mil-gra-na). L. " Millia " (thousands);

"grana" (seeds); from its many seeds. Eng.
name "Allseed." Second bot. name.

Militaris (mil-i-tar-is). L. adj., "military"; because
the flower is supposed to be like a helmet. Second
bot. name.

Mimulus (mim-u-lus). G. "Mimos" (a mimic). Bot.
name for a group.

Miniatum (min-i-a-tum). L. adj., "covered with red
lead"; *i.e.*, of a dingy red colour. Second bot.
name.

Minor (mi-nur). L. adj., "smaller."

Minimus (min-e-mus). L. adj., "smallest." Both of
these very common second bot. name for various
plants.

Mint. Eng. for Mentha (which see).

Minus (mi-nus). L. adj., "less." Second bot. name
for plants of different families.

Mistletoe (miz-zl-to). A.S. "Mistel-tan"; *i.e.*, "mis-
tel" (birdlime); "tan." (a twig). Eng. name for
a group and family.

Mite.

Mitis (mi-tis). L. adj., "mild or mellow." Second bot.
name.

Mithridate (mith-re-date). Name given by herbalists
to a compound of some 70 herbs, which was a supposed antidote to all poisons. It gets its name
from Mithridatis, King of Pontus, who is credited
with its discovery. Plants used in making the mix-
ture are known as Mithridate.

Mixta (miks-ta). L. adj., "intermingled." A second
bot. name applied by some botanists to a plant
thought to be not quite pure, but a variety of some
other.

Moenchia (mo-en-chi-a). After Moench, a botanist, Hesse Cassel, died 1829. Bot. name of a group.

Molle (mol-le). L. adj., " soft." Second bot. name for many plants of different families.

Molinia. After Molinia, a Chilian botanist, died 1829. Bot. name for a group; also a second bot. name.

Mollissima (mol-lis-si-ma). L. adj., " most soft." Second bot. name of a few plants of different families.

Molliformis (mol-li-for-mis). L. " Mollis " (soft); " formis " (shape). Second bot. name.

Mollugo (mol-lu-go). L. " Mollis " (soft); from the softness of the leaves. Second bot. name.

Monensis (mon-en-sis). L. The Roman name " mona " was applied to Anglesey; it looks as if wrongly applied to the Isle-of-Man, which in Welsh was " Manaw." Second bot. name for the Isle-of-Man Brassica.

Monoses (mon-os-es.) G. " Monos " (alone). A first or group name, used by some botanists for One-flowered Wintergreen.

Moneywort. Eng. translation of Nummularia (which see).

Monks Hood. The common Eng. name for Aconite, which it gets from the upper part of the flower being like the cowl of a monk.

Monocotyledon (mon-o-kot-e-le-don). G. " Monos " (one); " kotuledon " (the hollow of a cup); used for the seed lobe, as seen in grasses. Bot. name for one of the two great divisions into which ALL plants are sub-divided.

Monogynia (mon-o-jin-ia). G. " Monos " (one);

"gune" (woman); the flower having only one
style. Second bot. name.

Monorchis (mon-or-kis). G. "Monos" (one); "orchis" (tuber); the plant having only one tuber.
Second bot. name Musk Orchis.

Monspeliensis (mon-spel-i-en-sis). Second bot. name.
for Annual Beadgrass.

Monotropa (mon-o-tro-pa). G. "Monos" (one);
"tropo" (turning); because all the flowers turn
the same way. Bot. name of a group.

Montana (mon-tan-a). L. adj., "belonging to the
mountains." Second bot. name applied to many
plants of different families.

Montia. After the Italian botanist Monti, died 1760.
Bot. name for a group.

Monticola (mon-ti-ko-la). L. "Monti" (of the mountain); "cola" (a dweller). Second bot. name.

Moonwort. Eng. translation of the second bot. name
"Lunaria," which it gets from the crescent shape
of the segments of its fronds. Eng. name of Botrychium group.

Morio (mor-io). G. "Moros" (foolish). The plant
was also known as Fool's Orchis. Second bot.
name Green-winged Orchis.

Morsus-Ranae (mor-sus-ran-e). L. "Morsus," (a
biting); "ranae" (of a frog). Second bot. name.

Moscatel (mos-ka-tel). Eng. name for Adoxa group.
Derived from G. "moschos," the name of the
animal from whom musk was obtained.

Moschatum (mos-ka-tum). G. adj., "musky." Second
bot. name.

Moschatellina (mos-ka-tel-len-a). G. "Moskos"
(musk); because the leaves of the plant when

crushed give a faint smell of musk. Second bot.
name for the Moscatel.

Mother Wort. Eng. name for Leonurus Cardiaca.
"The powder thereof to the quantity of a spoon-
ful, drank in wine, is a wonderful help to women
in their sore-travail, as also for the suffocating, or
risings of mother; for these effects it is likely it
took the name of Motherwort with us."

Mousetail. Eng. translation of "myosurus," (which
see).

Mucronatus (mew-kro-na-tus). L. adj., "pointed." A
second bot. name.

Mucronulatus (mew-kro-nul-a-tus). L. diminutive of
above; also used as a second bot. name.

Mugwort. Eng. name for Artemisia Vulgaris. The
plant, being a specific for women's ailments, was
in A.S. called " Maegwort," *i.e.*, "maidswort,"
but as it was also used for flavouring ale, and as
such was put into "mugs," in time "maeg" was
corrupted into "mug."

Mulgedium (mul-ji-di-um). L. "Mulgeo" (to milk);
because of the milky juice of the plant. Is the first
or group name of some botanists for Alpine Lettuce.

Mullein (mul-en). Eng. name for Verbascum group;
said to be some corruption of L. "mollis" (soft),
which was given to the plant because of the soft
flannelly feel of the leaves.

Multicaulis (mul-ti-kaw-lis). L. "Multi" (many);
"caulis" (stalks). Second bot. name.

Multiflora (mul-ti-flo-ra). L. "Multi" (many); "flora"
(flowers). Second bot. name.

Muralis (mu-ra-lis). L. adj.; "on walls" from the

plants growing there. Second bot. name for plants
of different families.

Muricata (mu-ri-ka-ta). L. adj., "like the murex," a
fish covered with sharp points. A second bot.
name.

Muricatum (mu-ri-ka-tum). L. See above. Second
bot. name for a variety Salad Burnet, because the
calyx, when ripe, has prickles.

Murimum (mu-ri-mum).

Murorum (mu-ro-rum). L. both, used as second bot.
name for different plants. Are derived from L.
word "for a wall."

Muscari (mus-ka-ri). L. adj., "pertaining to flies."
Bot. name for a group.

Muscifera (mus-ki-fer-a). L. "Musca" (a fly); "fera"
(a bearer). Second bot. name Fly Orchis.

Muscosa (mus-kos-a). L. "Muscos" (moss); *i.e.*,
mossy. Second bot. name.

Mushroom (mush-room). A.S. "Maes" (a field);
"rhum" (a knob); *i.e.*, field knobs.

Mustard. Eng. name for several plants, chiefly belonging to Brassica group. The Eng. "mustard" and
the French "moutarde" are corruptions of
"mustem ardens" (hot must). The French pre-
pare their mustard with the must of wine.

Mutabilis (mu-tab-il-is). L. adj., "changeable."
Second bot. name.

Myosote (mi-o-so-te). Eng. rendering of Myosotis.

Myosotis (mi-o-so-tis). G. "Mus" (a mouse); "otes"
(an ear); *i.e.*, mouse-eared; because its leaves are
so shaped. Bot. name of group.

Myosurus (mi-o-su-rus). G. "Mus" (a mouse);

" oura " (a tail); the end of the pod like a mouse's tail. Bot. name of a group.

Myrica (mi-re-ka). G. for the Tamarisk. Bot. name for Gale group.

Myriophyllum (mi-re-o-fil-lum). G. " Myrio " (10,000); " phullon " (leaved); *i.e.*, many-leaved. Bot. name Water Milfoil group.

Myrrhis (mir-ris). G. " Murrha " (myrrh); from the smell of the leaf. Bot. name Ciceley group.

Myrsinites (mir-sin-i-tes). L. name for some plant derived from a G. word meaning " wine flavoured with myrtle." Second bot. name Whortle Willow.

Myrtillus (mir-til-lus). L. adj., " little myrtle." Second bot. name.

Myrtilloides (mir-til-loi-des). G. adj., " myrtle like." Second bot. name.

Myurus (mi-ur-us). G. " Mus " (a mouse); " ours " (tail). Second bot. name for Rat-tail Fescue Grass family.

N

Naiadeae (na-yad-e). L. name for " water nymphs." Bot. name for a family.

Nais (na-i-as). L. for " water nymph." Bot. name for Naiad group.

Nana (na-na). L. " Nanus " (a male dwarf); " nana " (female dwarf). Second bot. name for a few plants of different families.

Napellus (nap-el-lus). L. diminutive of " napus " (a turnip); from the shape of the root. Second bot. name.

Napus (na-pus). L. " Napus " (a turnip). Second bot. name for cultivated variety of Field Brassica.

11

Narcissus (nar-sis-sus). G. name of plant from
"narkao" (to deaden); because of its narcotic properties. Bot. name for a group.

Nardus (nar-dus). G. name for plant because its blossom is like ear of corn. Bot. name Mat-grass
group.

Narthecium (nar-the-si-um). G. name for some Umbelliferous plant with pithy stalks—the pith removed made a case for ointments. Bot. name for
a group.

Nasturtium (nas-tur-she-um). L. "Nasus" (the nose);
"tortus" (twisted); because on smelling the flower
its smell is so pungent that one's nostrils twist.
Bot. name for Water Cress group.

Natans (na-tans). L. adj., "floating." Second bot.
name for some plants whose leaves float on the
water.

Navel Wort. Translation of second bot. name "Umbilicus." See Pennywort.

Neapolitanum (ne-a-pol-i-ta-num). L. "of Naples."
Second bot. name applied sometimes to Common
Cyclamen.

Neglecta (neg-lekt-a). L. adj., "neglected." Second
bot. name.

Nemoralis (nem-or-a-lis).

Nemorosum (nem-or-o-sum).

Nemorum (nem-or-um). L. All three, having different
shades of meaning, are derived from L. word
"nemus" (a wood with open glades and meadows
for cattle). Second bot. name applied to plants of
different families.

Neottia (ne-ot-tia). G. "Neo" (new); "Tinea" (L.
for "a moth.") Tinea was the old name for the

plant, but was also the name of a genus of moths; to distinguish between them, the addition of "neo" was made to the plant's name.

Neotinea (neo-tin-ea). (See above.) Is first bot. name of some botanists for Dense-spiked Habenaria, Orchid family.

Nepeta (ne-pe-ta). An Egyptian word for a drug that "removed sorrow." It also meant a scorpion, and was said to cure its sting. Bot. name for a group.

Nephrodium (nef-rod-i-um). G. "Nephros" (a kidney); from the shape of the spore-cases of the fern. Group name of some botanists for many of the Shieldfern group.

Nettle. A.S. "Netele." Eng. name for Urtica group, but is not confined to this group, for plants of Lamium group are called "Dead Nettle." The Nettle is one of the five bitter herbs to be partaken by the Jews at the Feast of the Passover.

Nidus-Avis (ni-dus a-veez). L. "Nidus" (a nest); "avis" (bird's). Second bot. name Bird's Nest Orchis, because the roots cross each and are entangled like the sticks in a crow's nest.

Niger (ni-jer).

Nigra (ni-gra).

Nigrum (ni-grum). L. adj., "black." Second bot. name for many different plants.

Nightshade. A.S. "Nihtscada." Eng. name given to three different plants—(1) Enchanter's Nightshade; (2) Deadly Nightshade; (3) Plain Nightshade. All are poisonous more or less, but the "deadly" one more.

Nigrescens (ni-gres-sens).

Nigricans (ni-grik-ans). L. Both adj., "turning black." Second bot. name for several plants.

Nigritellus (ni-grit-el-lus). L. "Niger" (black); "tellus" (earth). Second bot. name.

Nipple Wort. Eng. name for Lapsana Communis; gets its name because, in the days of the herbalists, the plant was used to give relief to the breasts of women.

Nissolia (nis-sol-ia). After French botanist Nissole, who died 1735. Second bot. name Grass Vetchling, Pea group.

Nitens (ni-tens).

Nitidum (ni-ti-dum). L. adj., "shinning." Second bot. name applied to several plants of different families.

Nitgrass. Eng. name for Gastridum Lendigerum. "Nit" (the egg of a small insect) is only a translation of "lens" (a louse's egg).

Nitidulum (nit-id-u-lum). L. adj., "somewhat trim." Second bot. name.

Nivalis (niv-a-lis). L. adj., "snowy." Second bot. name.

Nobilis (no-bil-is). L. adj., "superior." Second bot. name.

Noctiflora (nok-ti-flo-ra). L. "Nox" (night); "flora" (flowers); *i.e.*, flowers at night. Second bot. name.

Nodiflora (no-di-flo-ra). L. "Nodus" (a knot); technically called a node; *i.e.*, point on stem where leaf bud breaks; "flora" (flowers). Second bot. name.

Nodosa (no-do-sa). L. adj., "full of nodes" (see above). Second bot. name.

Noli-Me-Tangere (no-li-me-tan-je-re). L. "Noli" (don't); "me" (me); "tangere" (touch); because when ripe the seeds are ejected from the pod on the slightest touch. Second bot. name for Yellow Balsam.

Non-Scriptus (non-skrip-tus). L. "Non" (not); "scriptus" (written). Second bot. name. See Agraphis.

Norvegicum (nor-ve-je-kum). L. for "Norwegian." Second bot. name.

Nuda (new-da). L. adj., "bare." Second bot. name.

Nudicaulis (new-de-kaul-is). L. "Nudus" (bare); "caulis" (stem). Second bot. name.

Nudiflorus (new-de-flo-rus). L. "Nudus" (bare); "florus" (flowers); because the plant does not flower until its leaves for the year have withered. Second bot. name Autumnal Crocus.

Nummularia (num-mul-ar-ia). L. "Nummus." G. name for a coin used in Sicily, because the look of the coin was like that of the leaf. Second bot. name Moneywort.

Nutans (new-tans). L. adj., "nodding" or "drooping." Second bot. name.

Nuphar (nu-far). Arabic name for Yellow Water-lily. Bot. name of group.

Nymphaea (nim-fe-a). G. "Nymphe" (goddesses of Springs). Bot. name for group.

Nymphaeaceæ (nim-fe-a-si-e). L. "Nymphaea" and "aceous" (like). Bot. name for Waterlily family.

Nymphaeoides (nim-fe-oi-des). G. "Nymphae" and "oides" (like); the leaves of the plant being like those of the Waterlily. Second bot. name.

O

Oak. A.S. " Ac." Eng. name for Quercus group.

Oat. A.S. "Ata." Eng. name for Avena group.

Obliquus (ob-leek-us). L. adj., " oblique." Second bot. name.

Oblongus (ob-long-us). L. adj., " longer than broad." Second bot. name.

Obovata (ob-o-va-ta). L. " Ob " and " ovate " (the opposite to egg-shaped); *i.e.*, the broad end upwards. Second bot. name.

Obscurus (ob-skew-rus). L. adj., " dark." Second bot. name.

Obtusa (ob-tu-sa). L. adj., " blunt or rounded at the end." Second bot. name.

Obtusangula (ob-tuse-ang-gul-a). L. " Obtusus " (blunt); " angula " (angled). Second bot. name.

Obtusifolium (ob-tus-i-fol-i-um). L. " Obtusus " (blunt); " folium " (leaf). Second bot. name.

Obtusiflorus (ob-tus-i-flo-rus). L. "Obtusus " (blunt); " florus " (flowered); *i.e.*, where the different pieces which go to make up the flower are all more or less blunted. Second bot. name.

Occidentalis (ok-si-den-tal-is). L. " for where the sun sets "; *i.e.*, the West. Second bot. name.

Ochroleucum (o-kro-lew-kum). G. "Ochro " (yellow); "-leucos " (white); *i.e.*, cream-coloured. Second bot. name.

Octopetala (ok-to-pet-al-a). G. " Octo " (eight); " petalon " (petals). Second bot. name.

Odorata (o-do-ra-ta). L. adj., " sweet-smelling." Second bot. name.

Odontites (o-don-ti-tes). G. ·"Odontos" (a tooth); because the plant was supposed cure for tooth-ache. Second bot. name.

Œnanthe (e-nan-the). G. "Oinos" (wine); "anthos" (flower); from the wine-like smell of the flower. Bot. name for a group.

Œnothera (e-no-the-ra). G. "Oinos" (wine); "thera" (getting); because the roots when dried get a wine-like smell. Bot. name of group.

Officinalis (of-fis-e-nal-is).

Officinarum (of-fis-e-nar-um). L. Both from "officina" (a shop or factory). The first of these two ·is one of the most common second bot. names, and was applied to all those plants which the herbalists—the druggists of days gone by—always kept in stock in their shops ready to supply to customers.

Old Man's Beard. Eng. name for Wild Clematis; so -called because when the seed is set, it is covered with a mass of curled long greyish hairs.

Oleaceæ (o-le-a-si-e). L. "Olea" (an olive); "aceous" (like). Bot. name of family.

Oleracea (o-le-ra-se). L. adj.; "herb-like"; from "olus" (kitchen vegetables, as cabbages, turnips, &c.). Second bot. name.

Oleifera (o-le-fera). L. "Olus" (a cabbage); "fera" (bearer). Second bot. name.

Oleifolia (o-le-fol-ia). L. "Olus" (a cabbage); "folia" (leaves). Second bot. name.

Olidum (o-li-dum). L. adj., "bad-smelling." Second bot. name.

Olitoria (o-li-tor-ia). L. "Belonging to the kitchen garden." Second bot. name.

Olusatrum (o-lus-atrum). L. "Olus" (a pot herb);

"atrum" (black); from the dark colour of the leaves. Second bot. name.

Onagraceae (on-a-jra-si-e). L. "Onager" (a wild ass); "aceous" (like). Bot. name Œnothera family.

Onion. From L. "unio" (a kind of single onion).

Onobrychis (on-o-bre-kis). G. "Onos" (an ass); "bruchon" (to bray); because an ass always brays for it. Bot. name Sanfoin group.

Ononis (on-o-nis). G. "Onos" (an ass); because he likes the plant. Bot. name for a group.

Onopordon (on-o-por-don). G. name for some kind of thistle. Bot. name of a group.

Opaca (o-pa-ka). L. adj., "in the shade." A second bot. name.

Ophioglossum (of-e-o-glos-sum). G. "Ophios" (a snake); "glossum" (a tongue); from the shape of the frond. Bot. name Adder's Tongue group.

Ophioglossifolius (of-e-o-glos-si-fol-ius). G. "Ophioglossum" and "folius" (a leaf); i.e., snake-tongue-leaved. Second bot. name.

Ophrys (of-ris). G. "for the eye-brow"; because G. ladies used the plant to darken their eyebrows. Bot. name for group.

Opium (o-pe-um). G. "Opion" (the juice of the poppy).

Oppositifolium (op-pos-it-i-fol-ium). L. "Oppositus" (opposite); "folius" (leaf); i.e., leaves are opposite to one another. Second bot. name.

Opulus (op-u-lus). L. name for some tree; now used as second bot. name for the Guelder rose.

Orache (or-atsh). French word for "mountain spinach." Now used as Eng. name for Atriplex group.

Oraria (or-a-ria). L. adj., "belonging to the coast." Second bot. name.

Orbiculare (or-bik-u-la-re). L. "A small orb or globe." Second bot. name.

Orchidaceæ (or-kid-a-si-e). L. "Orchid" and "aceous" (like). Bot. name for a family.

Orchis (or-kis). G. A word that describes the shape of the bulb. Bot. name for a group.

Oreopteris (or-e-op-ter-is). G. "Oreo" (a mountain); "pteris" (a fern). Second bot. name.

Orientale (o-re-en-ta-le). L. adj., "eastern"; *i.e.*, where the sun rises. Second bot. name.

Origanum (or-i-ga-num). G. "Oreo" (a mountain); "ganos" (beauty). Bot. name Marjoram group.

Ornithogalum (or-nith-o-ga-lum). G. "Ornithos" (a bird); "gala" (milk). Bot. name for a group.

Ornithopus (or-nith-o-pus). G. "Ornithos" (a bird); "pous" (a foot); from the shape of the pods, which look like a bird's foot. Bot. name for Bird's Foot group.

Ornithopodioides (or-nith-o-pod-io-des). G. "Ornithopodi" (see above) and "oides" (like). Second bot. name of some botanists for Birdsfoot Trigonel.

Oroabranchaceæ (or-o-ab-ran-ka-se-e). G. "Orobos" (a vetch); "ancho" (to strangle); parasitical plants living on the roots of other plants. Bot. name Broomrape family.

Orobanche (or-o-ban-ke). G. (See above). Bot. name Broomrape group.

Orobus (or-o-bus). G. name for Bitter Vetch. Second bot. name Upright Vetch. Orobus was a group name with Linneus.

Orpine (or-pin). Eng. name for one of the Stonecrop

group. Is a contraction of " orpiment " (the name
of a yellow metal), and was given because some of
the flowers are yellow. The same thing happens
with the name Chrysanthemum.

Orontium (or-on-ti-um). Old name for the Snapdragon.
Now second bot. name for Lesser Snapdragon.

Oryzoides (o-ri-zoi-des). G. " Oryza " (rice); " oides "
(like). Second bot. name.

Osier (o-zhe-er). From the French " osier " (a willow);
the word is usually applied to the long slender
shoots used for basket-making. Is now Eng. name
for Salix Viminalis.

Ossifragum (os-si-fra-gum). L. " Ossi " (a bone);
" fragum " (breaker); because the bones of sheep
feeding on the plants become brittle and easily
break. Second bot. name Bog Asphodel.

Osmunda (oz-mund-a). After Osmunder (the God
Thor). Bot. name Osmund group.

Ostruthium (os-truth-i-um). Old name for some plant;
now second bot. name for Masterwort.

Otites (o-ti-tis). G. " Ous " (the ear); from ear-like
shape of the leaf. Second bot. name.

Ovata (o-va-ta). L. adj., " egg-shaped." Second bot.
name.

Ovalis (o-va-lis). L. adj., " oval." Second bot. name.

Ovina (o-vi-na). L. adj., " belonging to a sheep."
Second bot. name.

Oxalis (oks-a-lis). G. word for " sour wine "; *i.e.*,
acid. Bot. name for group.

Oxyacantha (oks-e-ak-an-tha). G. " Oxus " (sharp);
" acantha " (a thorn). Second bot. name for Hawthorn.

Oxyacanthoides (oks-e-ak-an-thoi-des). G. " Oxya-

canth " (see above) and " oides " (like). Second
bot. name.

Oxycoccos (oks-e-kok-kos). G. "Oxus" (acid);
" coccos " (a berry). Second bot. name Crane-
berry.

Oxylepis (oks-e-le-pis). G. "Oxus " (sharp); " lepis "
(a scale). Second bot. name.

Oxlip. A.S. "Oxan-slyppe" (ox droppings) (see Cowslip). Common Eng. name for one of Primroses.

Oxyptera (oks-e-tera). G. "Oxus " (sharp); " pteron "
(winged). Second bot. name.

Oxyria (oks-e-ria). G. "Oxus " (sharp); from the
acid taste of the plant. Bot. name for a group.

Oxytropis (oks-e-tro-pis). G. " Oxus " (sharp); " tro-
pis " (keel); because the plants have a sharp
" keel," as the lower petals of the Peaflower are
called. Bot. name for a group.

P

Padus (pa-dus). L. name of river Po. Second bot.
name for Birdcherry.

Pæonia (pe-o-ni-a). G. After Pæon, a Greek
physician. Bot. name for a group.

Pæony (pe-o-ne). Eng. for above.

Paganum (pa-ga-num). L. adj., " belonging to the
village." Second bot. name.

Paigle (pa-gl). Eng. name for the Cowslip; from the
French " epingle " (a pin), because the style with
its stigma looks like a pin with a good head.

Paleaceum (pale-a-se-um). L. adj., " getting pale."
Second bot. name.

Pallens (pal-lens). L. adj., "pale coloured." Second bot. name.

Pallescens (pal-les-sens). L. adj., "growing pale." Second bot. name.

Pallidus (pal-li-dus). L. adj., "pale." Second bot. name.

Pallidiflora (pal-li-de-flo-ra). L. "Pallidus" (pale); "flora" (flowers). Second bot. name.

Palmata (pal-ma-ta). L. adj., "marked like a hand"; *i.e.*, when the lobes or veins of the leaf are spread out like fingers of the hand. Second bot. name.

Paludosa (pal-u-do-sa). L. adj., "boggy." Second bot. name.

Palustris (pal-us-tris). L. adj., "pertaining to a marsh." A very common second bot. name applied to plants of all families.

Pampinous (pam-pin-ous). L. adj., "full of leaves." Second bot. name.

Pampas Grass. Means the "grass of the plains," Pampa being the Peruvian word for a plain.

Panicea (pan-ik-e-a). L. adj., from "panicum" (which see). Second bot. name for Carnation Grass.

Panicle (pan-i-kl). A botanical term describing the way some flowers grow on plants, as seen in oats and grasses.

Paniculata (pan-ik-u-la-ta). L. diminutive of "panus" (a tuft or panicle). Second bot. name.

Panicum (pan-ik-um). L. name of a millet used for breadmaking. Bot. name for a group.

Pansy. Eng. name for a well-known flower, Violet group; from the French "pensee" (thought).

Pantothryx (pan-to-thriks). G. "Pante" (in every way); "thryx" (three-fold). Second bot. name.

Papaver (pa-pav-er). Celtic. "Papa," the seeds being used in the "pap" given to infants to induce sleep. Bot. name for Poppy group.

Papaveraceæ (pa-pav-er-a-se-e). L. "Papaver" (see above) and "aceous" (like): Bot. name for Poppy family.

Papilionaceæ (pa-pil-yo-na-se-e). L. "Papilio" (a butterfly); "aceous" (like); from the shape of the flowers. Bot. name Peaflower family.

Paradoxa (par-a-doksa). G. "Para" (against); "doxa" (usual opinion); i.e., doubtful. Second bot. name.

Paralias (par-a-li-as). G. adj., "grows on the sea-shore." Second bot. name.

Pardalianches (pard-al-i-an-kes). G. "Pardalis" (a leopard); "ancho" (to strangle); the plant was said to choke the leopard. Second bot. name Leopard's-bane.

Parietaria (pa-ri-et-ar-ia). L. adj., "pertaining to walls"; because plants usually found there. Bot. name Pellitory group.

Parietarifoliae (pa-ri-et-ar-i-fol-i-e). L. "Parietaria" (see above) and "folia" (leaves); i.e., leaves of the plant like those of the Wall Pellitory. Second bot. name.

Paris (pa-ris). L. adj., "equal"; because the four leaves are all the same and equal in size. Bot. name Herb Paris group.

Parnassia (par-nas-sia). After Mount Parnassus, where this Grass grows well. Bot. name for a group.

Parsley. Eng. name of a well-known garden herb. Is a corruption of G. "petroselinum." The second bot. name of one of the Carums. It is often used with other names, as Fool's Parsley, Hedge Parsley, Milk Parsley and Parsley Piert.

Parsnip. A corruption of and Eng. for L. "Pastinaca."

Parthenium (par-then-i-um). G. name applied to several plants. Second bot. name for Ferfew Chrysanthemum.

Parviflora (par-vi-flo-ra). L. "Parvus" (small); "flora" (flowered). Second bot. name.

Parvifolia (par-vi-fol-ia). L. "Parvus" (small); "folia" (leaved). Second bot. name.

Parvulus (par-vu-lus). L. diminutive of "parvus" (small). Second bot. name.

Pasque Flower (pask-flower). From the French word for Easter; the petals of the flower give a rich green colour, with which Easter eggs used to be stained. Eng. name for Anemone Pusatilla.

Passerina (pas-ser-e-na). L. adj., "fit for sparrows." Second bot. name.

Pastinaca (past-in-a-ka). L. for "parsnip." Bot. name for Parsnip group.

Patens (pa-tens). L. adj., "spreading out." Second bot. name.

Patula (pa-tu-la). L. adj., standing open." Second bot. name.

Pauciflora (paw-si-flo-ra). L. "Paucus" (few); "flora" (flowers). Second bot. name.

Pea. Eng. name for Lathyrus group.

Pearlwort. Eng. name for Sagina group.

Pear. Eng. name for Pyrus Communis. Pear in A.S. is "pera."

Pecten (pek-ten). L. for " a comb." Second bot. name for Venus' Comb or Shepherd's Needle.

Pectinatus (pek-tin-a-tus). L. adj., "sloped two ways as is a comb." Second bot. name.

Pedicellata (ped-is-el-la-ta). L. dim. of " pedis " (a foot); *i.e.*, having but a little foot-stalk. Second bot. name.

Pedicularis (pe-dik-u-la-ris). L. adj., " pertaining to lice "; because the plant was said to cause lice in sheep feeding upon it. Bot. name for a group.

Pedunculata (pe-dun-ku-la-ta). L. adj., formed from the botanical term " peduncle " (the single stalk of a flower), to distinguish it from " pedical " (the stalk of a bunch of flowers). Second bot. name.

Pellitori (pel-i-tor-i). A corruption of the L. " parietaria." Eng. name for that group of the Nettle family.

Peltatum (pel-ta-tum). L. adj., " armed with a crescent-shaped shield." Second bot. name.

Pelisseriana. After Pelisser. Second bot. name for Pelisser's Linaria.

Pencillatus (pen-sil-la-tus). L. adj., " small pencil like." Second bot. name.

Pendula (pen-du-la). L. adj., " hanging down." Second bot. name.

Pennycress. Eng. name for Thlaspi group. Gets " penny " from the flat penny-like pods of the plant.

Pennyroyal. Eng. name for Mentha Pulegium. Its " penny " has nothing to do with the coin of that name. In days of old it was known as Pulioleriall, evidently a corruption of Pulegium, its L. name.

Pennywort. Eng. name for a group (Hydrocotyle) and a plant (Cotyledon, Umbilicus), and owes its "penny," in both cases, to the round, penny-like look of the leaf.

Pentandrum (pen-tan-drum). G. "Pente" (five); "andrum" (men); *i.e.*, five stamened. Second bot. name.

Peplis (pep-lis.) G. name for one of the Spurges, but now used as bot. name of a group.

Peploides (pep-loi-des). G. "Peplis" (see above); "oides" (like). Second bot. name.

Peplus (pep-lus). G. Another form of "peplis." Second bot. name.

Peregrina (per-e-gri-na). L. adj.; "comes from foreign parts." Second bot. name.

Pepper. Eng. rendering of "Piperita" (which see).

Perennis (pe-ren-nis). L. adj., "lasts whole year through." Second bot. name.

Perfoliata (per-fol-i-a-ta). L. "per" (through); "folium" (the leaf); when the stalk looks as if it came through the leaf. Second bot. name.

Perforatum (per-for-a-tum). L. adj., "pierced through"; as if with little holes, like St. Johns-wort leaves. Second bot. name.

Perianth (per-i-anth). A botanical term. G. "Peri" (around); "anthos" (flower); *i.e.*, the envelope enclosing both the calyx (flower-cup) and petals, which surround true flower, *viz.*, stamens and pistils.

Periclymenum (per-i-kli-men-um). G. "Peri" (about); "clyneo" (to twine). Second bot. name Common Woodbine.

Periwinkle (per-i-wink-l). Eng. name for Vinca group.

"Winkle" is merely a corruption of L. "vinca." L. name of plant Perivinca.

Permixt (per-miks-ta). L. adj., "confusedly mixed." Second bot. name.

Perpusillus (per-pus-il-lus). L. adj., "very small." Second bot. name.

Persica (per-si-ka). L. name for the "peach." Was derived through the G. from the Persian name for the tree. Second bot. name.

Persicifolia (per-si-ki-fol-ia). L. "Persica" and "folia" (a leaf); *i.e.*, leaf like that of the Peach. Second bot. name.

Persicaria (per-si-ka-ri-a). L. adj., "peach-like"; from the leaf of plant being like that of the Peach. Second bot. name.

Petasites (pet-as-i-tes). G. "Petasos" (a sunshade); from the large size of the leaf of the plant. Second bot. name.

Petraea (pet-ra-e). L. "Petra" (a rock). Second bot. name.

Petroselinum (pet-ro-sel-i-num). G. "Petro" (a rock); "selinon" (parsley). Second bot. name.

Petty Whin. A second Eng. name for Needle Genista. Quite a different group from Ulex, the group of the Whin proper.

Peucedanum (pew-si-da-num). L. name for Hog's Fennel. Bot. name for a group.

Peucedanifolia (pew-si-da-ni-fol-ia). L. "Peucedani" (see above); "folia" (a leaf). Second bot. name.

Phaca (fa-ka). G. "Phakos" (a lentil), which was eaten chiefly at funerals. Group name of some botanists for Astragalus Danicus.

Phaeostachya (fa-o-sta-ke-a). G. "Phaeo" (brown);

"stachys" (a spike or ear of corn). Second bot. name.

Phaeum (fa-e-um). G. adj., "brown or swarthy." Second bot. name.

Phalaris (fa-la-ris). G. "Phalos" (shining); from the glossy look of seeds. Bot. name for group.

Phalaroides (fal-ar-oi-des). G. "Phalaris" (which see); "oides" (like). Second bot. name.

Pheasant's Eye. Eng. name for Adonis Autumnalis. Gets this name from bright red corolla and dark centre of flower.

Phegopteris (feg-o-ter-is). G. "Phego" (a beech tree); "pteris" (a fern). Second bot. name for Beechfern.

Phellandrium (fel-land-ri-um). G. name for a plant with ivy-like leaves. Second bot. name.

Philonotis (filo-no-tis). G. "Philo" (a lover); "notis" (of damp). Second bot. name.

Phleum (fle-um). G. name for some marsh plant. Now bot. name group.

Phoenica (fo-en-e-ka). L. adj., "blood-red"; from colour of petals. Second bot. name.

Phragmites (frag-mi-tes). G. adj., "of or for a fence." Second bot. name Com. Reed.

Phyllodoce (fil-lo-do-se). The name of one of Cyrene's water nymph attendants. Group name of some botanists for Blue Menziesia.

Physospermum (fi-so-sper-mum). G. "Phusa" (a bladder); "sperma" (a seed); the seed being in a loose cover. Bot. name of group.

Phylicifolia (fil-e-se-fol-ia). G. "Phylike" (name of an evergreen shrub; "folia" (L., a leaf); *i.e.*, phylica-like leaves. Second bot. name for Tea-leaved Willow.

Phyteuma (fi-teu-ma). G. "Phyton" (that which grows as a plant, a tree). Bot. name Rampion group.

Picea (pi-se-a). L. "Pix" (name for the Spruce tree).

Picris (pik-ris). G. "Pikros" (bitter); from taste of plant. Bot. name for a group.

Picrides (pik-ri-des). Second bot. name variety Lesser Broomrape, because this parasitic plant grows on the Picris plants.

Parsley Piert. Eng. name Alchemilla Arvensis.

Pig Nut. Eng. name for two plants of different groups —one belongs to Carum group; the other to Cono-podum.

Pillwort. Eng. name translation of "Pilularia," L. group name.

Pilulare (pil-u-la-re). L. "A little ball." Second bot. name.

Pilularia (pil-u-la-ri-a). L. "Pilula" (a little pill). Bot. group name.

Pilosus (pi-lo-sus). L. adj., "hairy." Second bot. name.

Pilosella (pi-lo-sel-la). L. adj. dim., "pilosus" (hairy), but the hairs are small. Second bot. name.

Pilosissimum (pi-lo-sis-si-mum). L. adj. superlative of "pilosus." Second bot. name.

Pilulifera (pil-u-li-fer-a). L. "Piluli" (a pill); "fera" (bearer); i.e., pill-headed. Second bot. name.

Pimpernel (pim-per-nel). Eng. name for Anagallis group. Said to be a corruption of "bipennella," a L. term applied to plants with feather-like leaves.

Pimpinella (pim-pin-el-la). L. Corrupted form of "bipinnula " (two feathered); *i.e.*, having, in pairs, two feather-like leaves along the stalk. Bot. name for group.

Pimpinellifolia (pim-pin-el-li-fol-ia). L. " Pimpinella " (see above); " folia " (leaves); *i.e.*, like those of the Pimpinella. Second bot. name.

Pimpinelloides (pim-pinel-loi-des). L. " Pimpinella " (see above); " oides " (like). Second bot. name.

Pine. Eng. rendering of L. " pinus " (name of tree).

Pinguicula (ping-u-ku-la). L. " Pinguis " (fat); from the greasy feel of the leaf. Bot. name of a group, and Eng. name for the Lentibulaceæ family.

Pink. Eng. name of Carophyllaceæ family, and Dianthus group is the short for Pinkstein or Pentecoste, when it flowers.

Pinus (pi-nus). L. name for Pine tree.

Pinnatum (pin-na-tum). L. adj., " feathered or plumed." Second bot. name.

Pinnatifieda (pin-nat-if-i-da). L. " Penna " (a feather); " findo " (to cleave); round its margin the leaf is cut in a jagged way half way down to midrib. Second bot. name.

Piperita (pi-per-e-ta). L. " Piper " (pepper); through Greek from Sanscrit " pippali." Second bot. name.

Pippin (pip-pin). Dutch. " Pipling." A distinguishing name given to one of the many kinds of apples.

Pisum (pis-um). L. name for Pea. Now used as the group name for cultivated kinds of Peas.

Planiculmis (pla-ni-kul-mis). L. " Planus " (flat); " culmis " (a stalk); flat-stemmed. Second bot. name.

Planifolia (pla-ni-fol-ia). L. " Planus " (flat); " folia " (leaves). Second bot. name.

Plantagineæ (plan-ta-gin-e-a). L. Bot. name for
Plantain family.

Plantaginea (plan-ta-gin-ea). L. adj., "plantain-like."
Second bot. name.

Plantago (plant-a-go). L. "Planta" (the sole of the
foot); from the shape of the leaf. Bot. name for
Plantain group.

Plantain (pla-tan). Eng. rendering of L. Plantago.

Platanus (plat-a-nus). L. name for Plane tree.

Platanthera (plat-an-thera). G. "Platus" (broad);
"anthros" (anther); the part of the stamen where
the pollen is. Second bot. name.

Platycarpa (plat-e-kar-pa). G. "Platus" (broad);
"karpos," (fruit). Second bot. name.

Platypetala (plat-e-pet-al-a). G. "Platus" (broad);
"petala" (petals). Second bot. name.

Platyphyllos (plat-e-fil-los). G. "Platus" (broad);
"phyllos" (a leaf). Second bot. name.

Platyptera (plat-e-tera). G. "Platus" (broad);
"ptera" (wings); the seeds of the plant being
broadly winged. Second bot. name.

Plicata (pli-ka-ta). L. adj., "doubled up." Second
bot. name.

Ploughman's Spikenard. Eng. name for Inula Conyza.
Spikenard is from L. "spica (a spike or ear);
"nard" (from the Sanscrit to smell); a highly
aromatic plant.

Plum. A.S. "Plume." Eng. name for a fruit tree.

Plumbagineæ (plum-ba-jin-e-e). Bot. name for Plumbago family.

Plumbago (plum-ba-go). L. name for Leadwort plant,
from "plumbum" (lead); referring to the colour
of the flower.

Plumaris (plum-ar-is). L. adj., " softly featherly." Second bot. name.

Pneumonanthe (nu-mo-nan-the). G. " Pneumon " (breath); " anthos " (flower); because of a peculiar arrangement of the corola tube. Second bot. name.

Poa (po-a). G. for " Grass.". Bot. name for a group.

Podagraria (po-dag-ra-ri-a). G. adj., " gouty "; the plant was said to be good for gout. Second bot. name.

Polemoniaceæ (pol-e-mo-ni-a-se-e). Bot. name for Polemonium family.

Polemonium (pol-e-mo-ni-um). G. " Polemos " (war); because two kings went to war as to which of them had discovered the virtues of the plant, at least, so Pliny says. Bot. name for a group.

Polita (po-li-ta). L. adj., " polished or smooth." Second bot. name.

Polifolium (po-li-fol-i-um). L. " Poli " (polished); " folium " (leaf). Second bot. name.

Pollen (pol-en). The fertilising powder contained in the anthers of flowers.

Polyanthus (pol-i-an-thus). Eng. name from G. " poly " (many); " anthus " (flowers); given to cultivated varieties of the Wild Primrose.

Polyanthemus (pol-i-an-the-mus). G. " Poly " (many); " anthos " (flowers). Second bot. name.

Polycarpon (pol-i-kar-pon). G. " Poly " (many); " karpos " (fruits). Bot. name for a group.

Polygala (pol-i-ga-la). G. " Poly " (much); " gala " (milk); from the milk-like juice of plant. Bot. name Milkwort group.

Polygalaceæ (pol-i-ga-la-se-e). Bot. name for Milkwort family.

Polygama (pol-i-ga-ma). G. "Poly" (many); "gama" (marriages); refers to the plants which have this description of flowers—male, female and hermaphrodite.

Polygonaceæ (pol-i-go-na-se-e). Bot. name Polygonum family.

Polygonatum (pol-i-gon-a-tum). G. "Poly" (many); "gonu" (joints); from the many joints of the stem. Bot. name for a group.

Polygonum (pol-i-gon-um). G. "Poly" (many); "gonu" (joints); from the many joints of the stem. Bot. name for a group of the Polygonum family. Polygonatum belongs to Lily family.

Polygonifolius (pol-i-go-ni-fol-ius). G. "Polygonum" and "folium" (a leaf); polygonum-like leaved. Second bot. name.

Polymorpha (pol-i-morfa). G. "Poly" (many); "morpha" (forms); i.e., very variable in appearance. Second bot. name.

Polynoda (pol-i-no-da). G. "Poly" (many); "nodus" (a knot). Second bot. name.

Polypodium (pol-i-po-di-um). G. "Poly" (many); "pous" (a foot); from the many rootlets thrown out along the root stock. Bot. name for a group.

Polypodiodes (pol-i-pod-i-o-des). G. "Polypodium" and "oides" (like). Second bot. name.

Polypogon (pol-i-po-gon). G. "Poly" (much); "pogon" (a beard); i.e., thick-bearded. Bot. name Beardgrass group.

Polyrrhiza (pol-i-ri-za). G. "Poly" (many); "rhiza" (a root). Second bot. name.

Polyspermum (poly-i-sper-mum). "Poly" (many); "spermum" (seeds). Second bot. name.

Polystachia (pol-i-sta-ki-a). G. " Poly " (many); " stachios " (spikes). Second bot. name.

Polystichum (pol-i-sti-kum). G. " Poly " (many); " stichos " (rows or ranks); refers to the seeds on the back of the frond. A group name used by some botanists instead of Aspidium for some Shieldferns.

Pomifera (pom-if-era). L. " Pomum " (fruit of any kind); " fera " (beare). Second bot. name.

Pondweed. Eng. name for Potamogeton group.

Poor Man's Weather Glass. Eng. name for Common Pimpernel; because of its sensitiveness for rain; the flower closes on the first signs of rain.

Poplar. Eng. rendering of L. " Populus." Name for a group.

Poppy (pop-i). Eng. name for Papaver (which see) group.

Populus (pop-u-lus). L. name for the Poplar tree. Bot. name of a group.

Porrum (por-rum). L. name for the Leek. Now used as second bot. name for the cultivated variety of the Wild Leek.

Porrifolius (por-ri-fol-i-us). L. " Porrum " and " folius " (a leaf). Second bot. name.

Portlandica (port-land-i-ka). L. adj., " belonging to Portland." Was the second bot. name given to Portland Spurge by Linneus.

Portula (port-u-la). L. A corruption of " portulaca." Second bot. name.

Portulaceæ (port-u-la-se-e). L. " Portulaca " (the name for Purslane); " aceous " (like). Bot. name Purslane family.

Portulacoïdes (port-u-lak-oi-des). G. " Portulaca "

and " oides " (like). Second bot. name Sea Purslane, Orache group.

Potamogeton (pot-am-og-et-on). G. " Potamos " (a
river); " geton " (a neighbour). Bot. name Pondweed group.

Potentilla (po-ten-til-a). L. " Potens " (powerful);
from its medicinal properties. Bot. name of a
group.

Poterium (po-ter-ium). L. form of G. " poterion " (a
drinking cup); the leaf of the plant, which has a
far-off taste of cucumber, was used in cooling
drinks. Bot. name of a group.

Praecox (pre-coks). L. adj., " early ripe." Second
bot. name.

Praelongus (pre-long-us). L. adj., " very long."
Second bot. name.

Pratensis (pra-ten-sis). L. adj., " found in the
meadows." A very common second bot. name
applied to all sorts of plants.

Prenanthes (pre-nan-thes). A group name of some
botanists for Wall Lettuce.

Prenanthoides (pre-nan-thoi-des). G. " Prenanth "
and " oides " (like). Second bot. name Prenanth
Hawkweed.

Primrose. L. " Primus," (first); from its early bloom-
ing. The " rose " has nothing to do with the
flower; it is an erroneous addition. Eng. name for
Primula group.

Primula (prim-u-la). L. " Primus " (first); *i.e.,* to
flower. Bot. name Primrose group.

Primulaceæ (prim-u-la-se-e). L. " Primula " and
" aceous " (like). Bot. name Primrose family.

Privet. Its old name was Primprint. Is the Eng. name for Ligustrum group.

Procumbens (pro-cum-bens). L. adj., "lying on the ground." Second bot. name.

Procurrens (pro-cur-rens). L. adj., "extending." Second bot. name.

Prolifer (pro-lif-er). L. "Proles" (offspring); "fer" (bearer); *i.e.*, produces an unusual number of buds. Second bot. name.

Pronus (pro-nus). L. adj., "leaning forward." Second bot. name.

Propinqua (pro-ping-kwa). L. adj., "near." Second bot. name.

Prostrata (pros-tra-ta). L. adj., "spread out." Second bot. name.

Pruinatum (pru-in-a-tum). L. "Pruina" (a hoar frost); from the look of the leaf. Second bot. name.

Pruinosa (pru-in-osa). L. See Pruinatum. Second bot. name.

Prunella (proo-nel-la). L. Brunella was the old spelling, but modern writers changed initial "B" into "P." Brunella was derived from German "braume" (quinsey), for which the plant was a cure. Bot. name for a group.

Prunifolia (prun-i-fol-ia). L. "Prunus" (a plum tree'; "folia" (leaf). Second bot. name.

Prunus (pru-nus). L. name for Plum tree. Bot. name for a group.

Psamma (sa-ma). G. "Psammos" (sand); because the plant grows on the sands of the sea-shore. Bot. name for group.

Psuedo (su-do). G. There are a number of compound words with this prefix, meaning "false." For the.

meaning of such compound word see second part
of the compound word under its own initial letter.

Ptarmica (tar-mik-a). G. " Ptarmos " (sneezing); the
dried leaves were used as snuff. Second bot. name.

Pteris (te-ris). G. name for a Fern, from " petron " (a
feather); because the leaf is feather-like. Bot.
name of group.

Pubens (pu-bens).

Puberula (pu-ber-u-la).

Pubescent (pu-bes-ent).

Pubigera (pu-bij-er-a). All are second bot. names, with
shades of difference in their meanings, derived
from L. " puber " (puberty); *i.e.*, clothed with soft
hair or down.

Pulegium (pu-lej-i-um). L. name for Penny Royal,
from L. " pulex " (a flea); the plant was said to
destroy fleas. Second bot. name.

Pulchella (pulkel-a). L. dim. of " pulcher " (beautiful).
Second bot. name.

Pulcher (pul-ker).

Pulchrum (pul-krum). L. adj., " beautiful." Second
bot. names.

Pulicaria (pul-i-kar-ia). L. name for plant, from L.
" pulex " (a flea). Second bot. name for Small
Fleabane.

Pulla (pul-a). L. adj., " dark coloured." Second bot.
name.

Pulmonaria (pul-mon-ar-i-a). L. " Pulmo " (the
lung); formerly a remedy for lung disease, because,
according to the law of signatures, the spots on
the leaves were supposed to represent diseased
lungs. Bot. name Lungwort group.

Pulsatilla (pul-sa-til-la). L. "Pulso." (to agitate).
Second bot. name.
Pulverulentum (pul-ver-u-len-tum). L. adj., "dusty";
from the look of the leaves. Second bot. name.
Pumalis (pu-ma-lis). L. adj., "dwarfish or small."
Second bot. name.
Punctata (punk-ta-ta). L. adj., "dotted." Second
bot. name.
Pungens (pun-gens). L. "Pungo" (to prick or sting).
Second bot. name.
Purpurata (pur-pu-ra-ta).
Purpurea (pur-pu-re-a).
Purpuroscens (pur-pu-ro-sens). All three with shades
of difference as to meaning; from a L. word for
"purple." Are used as second bot. names.
Purslane (purs-lan). Eng. name for Portulaceae
family. A corruption, through Italian, of L. name.
There are two plants belonging to two different
families; one to Pink, the other to Goosefoot. Both
known as Sea Purslane.
Pusilla (pu-sil-la). L. adj., "very little or petty."
Second bot. name.
Pycanthemum (pik-an-the-mum). G. "Puknos."
(thick); "anthos" (flower). Second bot. name.
Pycnocephalus (pik-no-se-fal-us). G. "Puknos"
(thick); "cephalus" (a head); *i.e.*, thick-headed;
as Composite flower-heads. Second bot. name.
Pygmaeus (pig-ma-us). L. from the G. name for
Pygmies of Central Africa; *i.e.*, dwarfish. Second
bot. name.
Pyramidalis (pir-a-mid-a-lis). L. adj., "pyramid-
shaped." Second bot. name.

Pyrenaica (pir-e-naika). L. adj., "belonging to the Pyrenees." Second bot. name.

Pyrethrum (pir-eth-rum). L. name for Pellitory. Also used by some botanists as group name for Fever-few Chrysanthemum.

Pyrola (pi-ro-la). L. "Pyrus" (a pear tree); because the leaf is like that of the Pear. Bot. name Winter-green group.

Pyrus (pi-rus). L. name for Pear tree. Bot. name for a group.

Q

Quadrangulum (kwod-rang-gu-lum). L. "Quator" (four); "angulum" (angles); *i.e.*, stalk is four-sided. Second bot. name.

Quadratum (kwod-ra-tum). L. adj., "square." Second bot. name.

Quake Grass. Eng. name for Briza group.

Quaternellum (kwor-ter-nel-lum). L. adj., "four each or by fours." Second bot. name.

Queen of the Meadows. Another Eng. name for Meadow Sweet.

Quercus (kwer-kus). L. name for the Oak. Bot. name for Oak group.

Quill Wort (kwil-wort). Eng. name for Isoetes group.

Quinquefida (kwin-kwe-fi-da). L. "Quinque" (five); "fida" (cleft). Second bot. name.

Quinquevulnera (kwin-kwe-vul-ner-a). L. "Quinque" (five); "vulnera" (notches). Second bot. name.

Quitch (kwich). A.S. "Cwic"; also called Couch. Eng. name for a well-known grass of Agropyrum group.

R

Racemosus (ra-sem-o-sus). L. adj., " full of clusters." Second bot. name.

Radiata (ra-di-a-ta). L. adj., " having rays "; refers to the minute rays of the outer florets of the flower. Second bot. name.

Radians (ra-di-ans). L. adj., " radiating from the centre." Second bot. name.

Radicans (rad-i-kans). L. adj., " striking roots "; *i.e.*, throws out rootlets from the main root. Second bot. name.

Radicata (rad-i-ka-ta). L. adj., " rooted "; *i.e.*, when the root is usually a long one. Second bot. name.

Radiola (rad-i-o-la). L. dim. of " radius " (the spoke of a wheel); because when ripe the fruit opens out and looks like the spokes of a small wheel. Bot. name Allseed group.

Radish. A. S. " Raedic." Eng. name for Raphanus group.

Radula (rad-u-la). L. dim. of " radix " (small rooted). Second bot. name.

Ragged Robin. Eng. name for Lychnis Flos-cuculi. Gets its " ragged " from its finely cut but ragged-looking petals.

Rag Wort. Eng. name of Senecio Jacobaea. Dedicated to St. James, patron of horses, because plant cured the staggers. Sometimes still known as Stagger Wort.

Ramosum (ram-o-sum). L. adj., " full of branches." Second bot. name.

Ramosissima (ram-o-sis-i-ma). L. adj. superlative of " ramosum "; *i.e.*, much-branched. Second bot. name.

Rampion (ram-pi-on). L. A corruption of "rapun-culus" (a small turnip). Eng. name for Phyteuma group. Was formerly cultivated for the root, which was eaten raw or boiled as a salad.

Ramps. A contraction of Rampion.

Ramsons (ram-zonz). A.S. "Hramsan." Eng. name for Allium Ursinum.

Ramulosa (ram-u-lo-sa). L. adj., "full of twigs." Second bot. name.

Ranunculaceæ (ra-nung-ku-la-se-e). L. "Ranuncu-lus" and "aceous" (like). Bot. name for a family.

Ranunculus (ra-nang-ku-lus). L. dim. of "rana" (a frog); because tadpoles love the damp places where these plants grow. Bot. name for a group.

Rapa (ra-pa). L. "Rapum" (a turnip). Second bot. name applied to Colza, a cultivated variety of Field Brassica.

Raphanistrum (raf-an-is-trum). L. "Raphanus" (which see); "istrum" or "astrum" added to another name shows that the plant is not quite the same, though somewhat like, the original. Second bot. name Wild Radish.

Raphanus (raf-a-nus). L. form of G. "raphnis," (a radish). Bot. name of Radish group.

Rapifera (rap-i-fera). L. "Rapa" and "fera" (a bearer). Second bot. name.

Rapum (ra-pum). L. "Rapum" (a turnip). Second bot. name.

Rapunculus (ra-pun-ku-lus). L. dim. of "rapum" (a little turnip); from the shape of the root. Second bot. name.

Rapunculoides (ra-pun-ku-loi-des). L. " Rapunculus," and " oides " (like). Second bot. name.

Rariflora (ra-ri-flo-ra). L. " Rarus " (not close nor thick); " flora " (flowers); *i.e.*, few flowered. Second bot. name.

Raspberry. Eng. name for Rubus Idaeus. Gets its "/rasp" from the rough appearance of the fruit. It was formerly called Hindberry.

Rattle. Eng. name for Rhinanthus group. Gets its name Rattle from the ripe seeds rattling in the pods.

Reclinata (rek-li-na-ta). L. adj., " reclining." Second bot. name.

Rectum (rek-tum). L. adj., " upright." Second bot. name.

Recurva (re-kur-va). L. adj., " curved back." Second bot. name.

Reed. A.S. " Hreod." Eng. name for Arundo group.

Reedmace. Eng. name for Typha group. Gets its name " Reedmace " because Rubens painted the Saviour holding this reed as a mace or sceptre in his hand.

Reflexum (re-fleks-um). L. adj., " bent back." Second bot. name.

Regalis (re-ga-lis). L. adj., " royal." Second bot. name of Fern Royal.

Remota (re-mo-ta). L. adj., " far apart "; refers to the spikelets of the plants, which are at some distance from one another. Second bot. name.

Reniformis (reni-for-mis). L. " Renes " (the kidneys); " forma " (shape); the leaves being kidney-shaped. Second bot. name.

Repens (re-pens). L. adj., "creeping." A common second bot. name for many plants.

Reptans (rep-tans). L. adj., "crawling." Second bot. name.

Reseda (re-se-da). L. "Resedo" (to soothe); from soothing medicinal effects of the plant. Bot. name Mignonette group.

Resedaceæ (re-se-da-se-e). L. "Reseda" and "aceous" (like). Bot. name for Mignonette family.

Restharrow. Eng. name for Ononis Arvensis. Said to get its Eng. name from its deep rooting stem causing the harrow to rest awhile.

Resupinatum (re-su-pin-a-tum). L. adj., "bent back"; because the side of the upper petal are turned outwards instead of inwards as with all other Clovers. Second bot. name for Reversed Clover.

Reticulata (ret-ik-u-la-ta). L. adj., "net-like"; refers to the way the veins of the leaves cross each other. Second bot. name.

Retusa (re-tu-sa). L. adj., "blunted." Second bot. name.

Rhamnaceae (ram-na-se-e). L. "Rhamnus" and "aceous" (like). Bot. name Buckthorn family.

Rhamnus (ram-nus). G. name for Blackthorn. Bot. name Buckthorn group.

Rhamnifolius (ram-ni-fol-i-us). L. "Rhamnus" and "folius" (leaved). Second bot. name.

Rhamnoides (ram-noi-des). G. "Rhamnus" and "oides" (like). Second bot. name.

Rhinanthus (ri-nan-thus). G. "Rhin" (a nose); "anthus" (a flower); from the nose-like look of

13

the upper lip of the flower. Bot: name Rattle group.

Rhodiola (ro-di-o-la). G. "Rodon" (a rose); because the root has a rose-like smell; hence its Eng. name Roseroot. Second bot. name.

Rhœas (re-as). G. name for Poppy. Second bot. name Field Poppy.

Rhynchospora (ring-kos-po-ra). G. "Rhynchos" (a snout); "spora" (seeds); i.e., where the fruit ends in a beak. Bot. name Beaksedge group.

Ribes (ri-bez). Arabic name for a kind of rhubarb, but now applied to Red and Black Currants. Bot. name for a group.

Ribesiaceæ (ri-bez-ia-se-e). L. "Ribes" and "aceous" (like). Bot. name for a family.

Rigidum (rij-i-dum). L. adj., "stiff." Second bot. name.

Rimosa (rim-o-sa). L. adj., "full of chinks." Second bot. name.

Riparius (ri-pa-ri-us). L. adj., "by river banks." Second bot. name.

Rivale (ri-va-le). L. adj., "belongs to a brook." Second bot. name.

Rivularis (riv-u-la-ris). L. adj., "belongs to a small brook." Second bot. name.

Roastbeef Plant. Eng. name for Iris Foetidissima, because of its smell.

Robertianum (rob-ert-i-an-um). Latinized "Robert," after St. Robert, Abbot of Molesme, and founder of Cistercian Order. Second bot. name for Herb Robert.

Robur (ro-bur). L. name for a hard Oak. Second bot. name British Oak.

Rockcress. Eng. name for Arabis group. "Cress" comes from L. "crescere" (to grow), because it grows very quickly.

Rocket (rok-et). Eng. name given to several plants; probably a corruption of Italian "Ruchetta," the name of one of them.

Rock Rose. Eng. name of Helianthemum group.

Roemeria (ro-mer-i-a). After Roemer, the botanist, died 1819. Second bot. name.

Romanzovianna. After Count Romanzoff, a Russian botanist. Second bot. name Drooping Lady's Tresses.

Romulea. Bot. name for a group.

Rosa (ro-sa). L. name for the "Rose." Bot. name for a group.

Rosaceæ (roz-a-sē-e). L. "Rosa" and "aceous" (like). Bot. name for Rose family.

Rosea (ros-ea). L. adj., "dewy," from "ros" (dew); because of the white mealy look of the leaf, as if it were covered with dew. Second bot. name.

Roseum (roz-e-um). L. adj., "rose-coloured." Second bot. name.

Rosemary (roz-ma-ri). A corruption of bot. name "Rosmarinus," meaning Sea-dew, from "ros" (dew) and "marinus" (of the sea); so named because it grows well on the sea-shore.

Roseroot. See Rodiola.

Rosmarinifolia (roz-ma-rin-i-fol-ia). L. "Rosmarinus" (rosemary); "folia" (leaf); i.e., rosemary-leaved. Second bot. name.

Rostellata (ros-tel-la-ta). L. adj., "having a little beak," the nut being beaked. Second bot. name.

Rostrata (ros-tra-ta). L. adj., "having a beak," the fruit has a long beak. Second bot. name.

Rotundifolia (ro-tund-i-fol-ia). L. "Rotundus" (round); "folia" (leaved). Second bot. name for many different plants.

Rowan Tree. Or Mountain Ash is the Eng. name for Pyrus Aucuparia. Rowan is derived from Norse "runa" (a charm); for the belief was that a piece of this sacred tree was an effective antidote to all evil spells.

Rubella (roo-bel-a).

Rubens (roo-bens).

Rubescens (roo-bes-ens). All three L. adj., from "rubeo" (to be red); means reddish; with shades of difference. Second bot. names.

Rubia (roo-bi-a). L. "Ruber" (red); from the roots of the plant is obtained Turkey-red dye. Bot. name Madder group.

Rubicolor (roo-bi-col-or). L. "Rubia" and "color" (colour). Second bot. name.

Rubiginosa (roo-bi-jin-o-sa). L. adj., "rusty"; from the colour of leaves. Second bot. name.

Rubrum (roo-brum). L. adj., "red or ruddy." Second bot. name given to several plants of different groups.

Rubus (roo-bus). L. name for the Bramble. Bot. name for a group.

Ruderale (roo-der-a-le). L. adj., "on mortar rubbish," where the plant thrives. Second bot. name.

Rudens (roo-dens). L. adj., "rough, uncultivated." Second bot. name.

Rue (roo). A corruption of "ruta," L. name for plant. Eng. name for a well-known herb.

Rufescens (roo-fes-ens). L. adj., "turning red." Second bot. name.

Rufus (roo-fus). L. adj., "red." Second bot. name.

Rugosa (roo-go-sa). L. adj., "wrinkled." Second bot. name.

Rumex (roo-meks). L. name for "sorrel." Bot. name Dock group.

Rupestris (roo-pes-tris). L. adj., "growing on rocks." Second bot. name.

Rupicola (roo-pi-co-la). L. adj., "rupis" (a rock) and "cola" (a dweller).

Ruppia (roop-pi-a). After Ruppius, German botanist, died 1719. Bot. name for a group.

Rupture Wort. Eng. name for Herniaria group.

Rurivagum (roo-ri-va-gum). L. "Rus" (the country); "vagum" (wandering about). Second bot. name.

Ruscus (rus-kus). Herbalists called it Bruscus, from "bruskelen," Celtic name for box-holly. Bot. name for a group.

Rush. Eng. name for Juncus group.

Rusticana (rus-tik-a-na). L. adj., "of the country." Second bot. name.

Rutabaga (roo-ta-ba-ga). Second bot. name Swedish Turnip, a cultivated variety of Field Brassica.

Rutaceum (roo-ta-se-um). L. adj., "rue-like," from L. "ruta" (rue). Second bot. name.

Ruta-muraria (roo-ta-mu-ra-ri-a). L. "Ruta" (rue); "muraria" (of the walls). Second bot. name.

Rye (ri). A.S. "Ryge." Name of a cereal, inferior to Wheat, but more hardly, and therefore cultivated in cold climate.

S

Sabaudum. Savoy in Latin dress. Second bot. name.

Sabulosa (sab-u-lo-sa). L. adj., " sandy "; the soil it loves. Second bot. name.

Sabulicola (sab-u-li-co-la). L. "Sabulus " (coarse gravel); " cola " (a dweller in). Second bot. name.

Saffron (saf-run). Arabic. " Zafaran." Are the dried stigmas (which see) of the Crocus. Meadow Saffron is an Eng. name for Colchicum.

Sage (saj). French. " Sauge." Eng. name for Salvia group.

Sagina (sa-ji-na). L. " Fattening food." Bot. name for Pearlwort group.

Saginoides (sa-jin-oi-des). L. " Sagina " and " oides " (like). Second bot. name.

Sagittata (saj-it-ta-ta). L. adj., " arrowish." Second bot. name.

Sagittaria (saj-it-ta-ri-a). L. " Sagitta " (an arrow); from the shape of the leaf. Bot. name Arrowhead group.

Sagittifolia (saj-it-ti-fol-ia). L. " Sagitta " (an arrow); " folia " (a leaf). Second bot. name.

Sainfoin (san-foin). Sometimes written Saintfoin, from French " sain " (holy) " foin " (hay); so called, " they " say, because it was the hay in the manger when the Saviour was born. Eng. name for Onobrychia group.

St. John's Wort. Eng. name for Hypericum. Gets its Eng. name because, according to old custom, it was on the eve of St. John's Day—24th June—that the plant was brought into the house as a charm to keep away evil spirits.

St. Patrick's Cabbage. Another Eng. name for London Pride. Gets its "Patrick" from growing in Ireland, for while found growing along Spain and Portugal, it also appears in W. and S.W. of Ireland.

Salad Burnet. Eng. name for Poterium Sanguis Orba. Called "salad" because its leaves have taste and smell of cucumber, and are therefore used in salads.

Salicaria (sal-i-ka-ria). L. "Willow-like"; the plant was formerly classed with the Willow-herbs. Second bot. name.

Salicifolia (sal-i-si-fol-ia). L. "Salix" (a willow); "folia" (leaves). Second bot. name.

Salicina (sal-i-si-na). L. "Willowy." Second bot. name.

Salicornia (sal-i-kor-ni-a). L. "Sal" (salt); "cornu" (a horn); from horn-like stem and large amount of soda it extracts from the soil. Bot. name Marsh Samphire group.

Saligna (sal-ig-na). L. "Willowy." Second bot. name.

Salina (sal-i-na). L. "Saltish." Second bot. name.

Salisburgensis (sal-is-bur-gen-sis). Salisbury in Latin dress. Second bot. name.

Salix (sa-liks). L. name for Willow. Bot. name for Willow group.

Sallow (sal-o). A.S. "Sealh." Eng. name for Salix Caprea.

Salsify (sal-si-fi). A corruption of Italian "sasefrica" (goat's beard), which in its turn is but a translation of the G. name for the plant. Eng. name for Tragopogon group.

Salsola (sal-so-la). L. " Sal " (salt), from the large quantity of soda the plant takes up out of the soil. Bot. name for Saltwort group.

Salsuginosus (sal-su-gin-o-sus). L. adj., " growing in places at times covered with brackish water." Second bot. name.

Saltum (sal-tum). L. " A leap or bound "; refers to the way the young shoots bend over and take root. Second bot. name.

Salt Wort. Salsola (which see).

Salvia (sal-vi-a). L. adj., " well or sound "; from the medicinal properties of the plant. Bot. name Sage group.

Sambucus (sam-bu-kus). L. name for the Elder. Bot. name of a group.

Sambucifolia (sam-bu-si-fol-ia). L. " Sambucus " and " folia " (leaves). Second bot. name.

Samolus (sam-o-lus). After the Island of Samos, where the plant was common. Bot. name of a group.

Samphire (sam-fir). A corruption of " San Pietro " (St. Peter), to whom the plant was dedicated. Eng. name for Crithmum group.

Sandal Wood. Sanscrit. " Chandana," name for the tree. Eng. name for a family.

Sand Spurry (spur-i). See Spurry. Eng. name for Spergularia group.

Sand Wort. Eng. name for and translation of bot. name of the group " Arenaria."

Sanguinale (sang-gwen-a-le). L. adj., " causing blood to flow "; *i.e.*, cuts the hand. Second bot. name.

Sanguineum (sang-gwen-e-um). L. adj., " blood-red," from L. " sanguis " (blood). Second bot. name.

Sanguisorba (sang-gwis-or-ba). L. ". Sanguis " -
(blood); " sorba " (to suck up); the leaves of the
plant stop bleeding. Bot. name of a group.

Sanicula (san-ik-u-la). L. " Sano " (to heal); from
the healing properties of the plant. Bot. name for
a group.

Santalaceæ (san-ta-la-se-e). L. " Santal," a corruption of Sanscrit " chandana; " aceous " (like).
Bot. name for a family. The sweet-smelling sandal
is obtained from a tree belonging to this family.

Saponaria (sap-o-na-ria). L. " Sapo " (soap); from
the juice of the leaves acting like soap. Bot. name
for a group.

Saracenicus (sar-a-sen-ikus). Arabic. " Sharq " (the
East); *i.e.*, Arabia. Second bot. name.

Sardous (sar-do-us). L. adj., " pertaining to Sar-
dinia." Second bot. name.

Sarmentaceae (sar-ment-a-se-e). L. adj., " inclined to
be full of twigs." Second bot. name.

Sarothamnus (sa-ro-tham-nus). G. " Saro " (to
sweep); " thamnos " (a bush); *i.e.*, besoms were
made from the plant. Some botanists use this as
a group name in place of " cytisus."

Sativus (sa-tiv-us). L. adj., " cultivated." A common
second bot. name applied to several different
plants.

Sauce Alone. Eng. name for Allaria Officinalis. Said
to be given from the leaves smelling so strong of
garlic as to be " sauce-alone " when eaten with
anything else.

Saussurea (saus-ur-ea). After Saussure, naturalist,
Geneva, died 1799. Bot. name for a group.

Savii. After Savi. Second bot. name.

Saw Wort. Eng. name for a group and translation of its bot. name L. " Serratula."

Saxatalis (sak-sa-ta-lis). L. adj., "found among rocks. Second bot. name.

Saxifraga (sak-si-fra-ja). L. " Saxum " (a rock); "fraga " (breaker); i.e., splits the rocks with its growing roots. Bot. name for a group.

Saxifragaceæ (sak-si-fra-ja-se-e). L. " Saxifraga " and " aceous " (like). Bot. name for a family.

Scaber (ska-ber).

Scabrum (ska-brum). L. adj., "rough." Second bot. names.

Scabiosa (ska-bi-o-sa). L. adj., " roughish." Bot. name for a group.

Scabriuscula (ska-bri-us-ku-la). L. adj., "slightly rough." Second bot. name.

Scales. A bot. term for small reduced leaves, which protect the dormant living germs of buds.

Scandix (skan-diks). G. name for Chervil. Now bot. name for a group.

Scandica (skan-de-ka). L. adj., "Chervil-ish." Second bot. name.

Scapigera (skap-ij-er-a). L. " Scapus " (a stem); " gero " (to bear). Second bot. name.

Scariola (skar-i-o-la). L. " A thorny shrub." Second bot. name.

Sceleratus (sel-er-a-tus). L. adj., "wicked "; from the extreme acridity of its sap. Second bot. name.

Scheuchzeria. After the brothers Sceuchzer, Swiss botanists. Bot. name for a group.

Schoberia (sko-ber-ia). Used as a group name by some instead of Suaeda.

Schoenus (ske-nus). G. name for a rush or reed. Bot. name for a group.

Schœnoprasum (ske-no-pras-um). G. "Schoenus" and "prasum," (a leek). Second bot. name for Chives.

Scilla (sil-a). G. "Skilla" (a sea-onion). Bot. name for a group.

Scirpus (sir-pus). L. name for Bulrush or rush without a joint. Bot. name for a group.

Sciuroides (si-u-roi-des). G. "Sciurus" (a squirrel); "oides" (like); *i.e.*, curved like a squirrel's tail. Second bot. name.

Scleranthus (skle-ran-thus). G. "Scleros" (hard); "anthos" (a flower). Bot. name for a group.

Sclerochloa (skle-ro-klo-a). G. "Scleros" (hard); "chloa" (grass). Group name by some botanists for some of the Pea group.

Sclerophylla (skle-ro-fil-la). G. "Sclero" (hard); "phylla" (leaves). Second bot. name.

Scleropoa (skle-ro-poa). G. "Scleros" (hard); "poa" (grass). Second bot. name.

Scolopendrium (skol-o-pen-drium). G. name for a centipede; applied to the plant because the lines of its seeds look like a centipede's feet. Bot. name Harts-tongue group.

Scoparius (sko-pa-ri-us). L. "A sweeper"; derived from a L. word meaning "thin branches." Second bot. name.

Scordium (skor-di-um). G. word for garlic. Second bot. name.

Scordonia (skor-do-ni-a). G. A contraction of "scordion" (garlic).

Scordoprasum (skor-do-pra-sum). G. "Scorodion"

(garlic); "prasum" (a leek). Second bot. name.

Scrophularia (skrof-u-lar-ri-a). L. "Scrofula," name of the disease for which the plant was a supposed remedy. Bot. name for a group.

Scrophularineæ (skrof-u-la-ri-ne-e). Bot. name for a family.

Scoticum (sko-ti-kum). Scotland in Latin dress. Second bot. name.

Scurvy Grass. Is not a grass. Eng. name for Cochlearia Officinalis.

Scytellata (sku-tel-la-ta). L. adj., "small salverish." Second bot. name.

Scutellaria (sku-tel-la-ri-a). L. "Scutella" (a small salver); from the shape of flower. Bot. name Skullcap group.

Scuticosa (sku-ti-ko-sa). L. adj., "like a lash or whip." Second bot. name.

Sea Kale. Eng. name for Crambe Maritima, found growing wild along the coast, now cultivated in gardens.

Secalinus (se-ka-li-nus). L. adj., "rye-like"; from L. "secale" (rye grass). Second bot. name.

Secunda (se-kun-da). L. adj., "second in order." Second bot. name.

Sedge (sej). A.S. "Secg." Eng. name for a family.

Sedoides (se-doi-des). L. "Sedum" and "oides" (like). Second bot. name.

Sedum (se-dum). L. "Sedeo" (to sit down); from the appearance of the plant wherever it may be growing. Bot. name Stonecrop group.

Segetum (se-ge-tum). L. "Seges" (a field of standing corn), where the plant is often found. Second bot. name.

Segetalis (seg-et-al-is). L. adj., "among the standing corn." Second bot. name.

Selago (se-laj-o). L. name for a kind of Club Moss. Second bot. name.

Selaginella (se-laj-i-nel-la). L. from "selago." Bot. name for a group.

Selaginelleæ (se-laj-i-nel-la-se-e). Bot. name for a family.

Selaginoides (se-laj-in-oi-des). L. "Selago" and "oides" (like). Second bot. name.

Self-Heal. Eng. name for Prunella, from its great reputation for medicinal properties.

Semidecandrum (sem-i-dec-an-drum). L. "Semi" (half); "dec" (ten); "andrum" (male); *i.e.*, five male flowers, instead of the usual ten. Second bot. name.

Sempervirens (sem-per-vir-ens). L. "Semper" (ever); "virens" (green). Second bot. name.

Sempervivum (sem-per-vi-vum). L. "Semper" (ever); "vivum" (living). Bot. name for Houseleek group.

Senebiera (sen-eb-i-era). After Senebier, a physiologist, of Geneva, died 1809. Bot. name for a group.

Senecio (se-ne-si-o). L. "Senex" (an old man); refers to the tufts of white hair attached to the seeds, and by which they are wafted about. Bot. name for a group.

Senescens (se-ne-sens). L. adj., "growing old." Second bot. name.

Sepium (se-pi-um). L. "Sepes" (a hedge), where the plant is often to be found. Second bot. name.

Sepincola (se-pin-co-la). L. "Sepes" (a hedge); "cola" (a dweller). Second bot. name.

Septangulare (sep-tang-gul-a-re). L. "Septem" (seven); "angulare" (angled); i.e., seven cornered. Second bot. name.

Septentrionale (sep-ten-tri-o-nale). L. "Septem" (seven); "triones" (ploughing oxen); i.e., the seven stars which form the Great Bear, close to the North Star, hence Northern. Second bot. name.

Serotina (se-rot-i-na). L. adj., "late in the season." Second bot. name.

Serpentini (ser-pent-i-ni). L. adj., "pertaining to a serpent." Second bot. name.

Serpyllum (ser-pil-lum). G. name for Wild Thyme. Now used as its second name.

Serpyllifolia (ser-pil-li-fol-ia). L. "Serpyllum" and "folia" (leaves); i.e., Thyme-leaved. Second bot. name.

Serpyllacea (ser-pil-la-se-a). L. "Serpyllum" and "aceous" (like). Second bot. name.

Serrafalcus (ser-ra-fal-kus). L. "Serra" (a saw); "falcus" (a sickle). Bot. or group name used by some instead of "bromus" for the Field Brome.

Serratula (ser-ra-tu-la). L. "A little saw"; from the margin of the leaf being toothed like a saw. Bot. name Saw Wort group.

Serratifolia (ser-ra-ti-fol-ia). L. adj., "saw-leaved"; from the margin of the leaf being toothed. Second bot. name.

Serratus (ser-ra-tus). L. adj., "saw-like"; i.e., leaves toothed like a saw. Second bot. name.

Service Tree. Eng. name for Pyrus Torminalis. The

word "service" is from a Gallic word, "cervisia," for beer, which used to be made from the fruit of the tree.

Seseli (ses-el-i). L. name for the plant. Bot. name for a group.

Sesleria (ses-ler-ia). After Sesler, Italian botanist. Bot. name for group.

Sessiliflora (ses-sil-i-flo-ra). L. "Sessilis" (sitting close), *i.e.*, having no stalk; "flora" (a flower). Second bot. name.

Setacea (se-ta-se-a). L. "Seta" (a thick, stiff hair); *i.e.*, a bristle. Second bot. name.

Setaria (se-ta-ria). L. "Seta" a bristle); from the bristles which cover the spikelets. A group name of some botanists for the Panicum group.

Setosa (se-to-sa). L. adj., "covered with bristles." Second bot. name.

Setter Wort. One of Eng. names for Fetid Hellebore.

Sexangulare (sek-sang-gu-la-re). L. "Sex" (six); "angulare" (angled); *i.e.*, six-cornered. Second bot. name.

Sheep's Bit. Eng. name for Jasione Montana.

Shepherd's Needle. One of Eng. names for Scandix Pecten; from its peculiar seed vessels, which grow in clusters of five or six, long and tapering to a point, have a needle-like look.

Shepherd's Purse. Eng. name for Capsella Bursa-Pastoris, and translation of its second bot. name. Gets its name from its little heart-shaped seed vessels, which resemble the old-fashioned pouch purse.

Shepherds' Weather Glass. Another name for Poor Man's Weather Glass (which see).

Sherardia (sher-ard-i-a). After Sherard, English botanist, died 1728. Bot. name for a group.

Shield Fern. Eng. name for and translation of Aspidium.

Sibbaldi (sib-bald-i). After Sibbald, Scottish botanist, died 1720. Second bot. name.

Sibiricum (si-bi-ri-kum). Siberia in Latin dress. Second bot. name.

Sibthorpia (sib-thorp-i-a). After Sibthorp, Eng. botanist. Bot. name of group.

Sieglingia (sej-ling-i-a). A group name used by some botanists instead of Triodia.

Siifolium (si-fol-i-um). L. "Sii" and "folium" (a leaf); *i.e.*, sii-leaved. Second bot. name.

Silaus (si-laws). L. name for some plant. Now used as bot. name of group.

Silaifolia (si-la-fol-ia). L. "Silaus" and "folia" (leaves). Second bot. name.

Silene (si-le-ne). G. "Sialon" (saliva); from the sticky juice which exudes from the plant for catching small insects. Bot. name of group.

Silver Weed. Eng. name for Potentilla Ansefina; from the silvery look of the underside of the leaves.

Silybum (si-lib-um). A group name used by some botanists for Carduus group.

Simethis (si-me-this). After a river in Sicily. Bot. name of a group.

Simia (sim-i-a). L. for "an ape." Second bot. name.

Simplex (sim-pleks). L. adj., "simple." Second bot. name.

Sinapis (si-na-pis). G. "Sinapi" (mustard plant). Second bot. name for Charlock or Wild Mustard. Many of the plants in the Brassica group have the

synonym " sinapis " because Linnœus had grouped
them under that name.

Sinapistrum (si-na-pis-trum). L. "Sinapis" (mustard);
" istrum." Second bot. name used by some
botanists for Charlock.

Sinuata (sin-u-a-ta). L. adj., "curved"; from the
margin of the leaves being wavely curved.. Second
bot. name.

Sison (si-son). A Celtic word for a running stream.
Bot. name of a group.

Sisymbrium (si-sim-bri-um). G. name for some similar
plant. Bot. name of a group.

Sisyrinchium (si-sir-ink-i-um). G. name for some
bulbous plant. Bot. name of a group.

Sium (si-um). Celtic. "Siw" (water). Bot. name of
a group.

Skull Cap. Eng. name for Scutellaria group; sometimes called, from the shape of the flower, Helmet-
flower.

Sloe. A.S. "Slag" (sour). Eng. name for the Blackthorn.

Small Reed. Eng. name for Calamagrostis group.
" Reed " is a translation of its bot. name
" Calama."

Smilacina (smil-a-si-na). L. dim., "Smilax." Used
by some botanists as a group name for May Lily.

Smithii (smith-i). After J. E. Smith, an Eng. botanist,
died 1828. Second bot. name.

Smyrnium (smir-ni-um). G. "Smurnia" (myrrh);
from the smell of the sap of the plant. Bot. name
of a group.

Snake's Head. Eng. name for Common Fritillary.

14

Snake Tongue. Is a translation of " Ophioglossum,"
part of the second bot. name for plant.

Snake Weed. Eng. name for Polygonum Bistorta.

Snapdragon. Eng. name for Antirrhinum group.

Sneeze Wort. Eng. name for Achillea Ptarmica.

Snowdrop. Eng. name for Galanthus group.

Snowflake. Eng. name for Leucoium group.

Soap Wort. Eng. name for a group and translation of
" Saponaria," its bot. name.

Solanaceæ (so-la-na-se-e). L. " Solanum " and
" aceous " (like). Bot. name for a family.

Solanum (so-la-num). L. name for Black Nightshade.
Now used for Solanum group.

Soldanella (sol-da-nel-la). Said to be from " soldo,"
an Italian coin, from the roundness of its leaf.
Second bot. name.

Solida (sol-i-da). L. adj., " solid." Second bot. name.

Solidago (sol-i-da-go). L. " Solido " (to unite); from
the medical properties of the plant. Bot. name
Golden-rod group.

Solomon-Seal. Eng. name for Polygonatum group.
Gets its name because on cutting the roots of the
plant there are marks like a six-pointed star formed
by the crossing of two triangles over each other,
and which the Arabs call " Solomon-Seal."

Solstitialis (sol-stit-i-al-is). L. adj., " belonging to the
summer months." Second bot. name.

Somniferum (som-nif-er-um). L. " Somnus " (sleep);
" ferum " (beare). Second bot. name Opium
Poppy.

Sonchus (son-kus). L. name for the plant. Second
bot. name Sow Thistle group.

Sophia (sof-i-a). G. " Sophos " (wisdom); so highly

was the plant valued by the herbalists of old that
they called it "the Wisdom of the Surgeons."
Second bot. name Flixweed.

Sorbus (sor-bus). L. name for Beam tree. Is used by
some botanists as group name instead of Pyrus.

Sorrel (sor-el). A.S. "Sur" (sour). An Eng. name
applied to several plants having this characteristic.

Sow Bread. Eng. name for Common Cyclamen, because where abundant forms the chief food of
swine.

Sow Thistle. Eng. translation of "Sonchus," the bot.
name.

Spadicea (spa-di-se-a). G. "Spadix" (palm branch).
Second bot. name.

Sparganium (spar-ga-ni-um). G. "Sparganon" (a
bandage). Bot. name of a group.

Sparsiflora (spar-si-fol-ia). L. "Sparsus" (spread
out); "flora" (flowers); i.e., flowers far apart.
Second bot. name.

Spartina (spar-ti-na). G. "Sparton" (a small cord).
The plant was used for withes. Eng. name Cord-
grass. Bot. name of a group.

Spathulata (spa-thu-la-ta). L. "Spathula" (a spoon);
the leaf being spoon-shaped. Second bot. name.

Spathulaefolius (spa-thu-le-fol-i-us). L. "Spathula"
(a spoon) and "folius" (a leaf). Second bot. name.

Spear Thistle. Eng. name for a Thistle, and translation of "lanceolatus," its second bot. name.

Spear Wort. Eng. name for Ranunculus Lingua; refers to shape of leaf.

Speciosa (spesh-i-o-sa). L. adj. Second bot. name.

Spectabilis (spek-tab-i-lis). L. adj., "visible." Second
bot. name.

Specularia (spek-u-la-ri-a). L. "Speculum" (a mirror); *i.e.*, shining; from the seeds being so bright. Group name of some botanists for Campanula Hybrida.

Speedwell. Eng. name for Veronica group. "Speedwell" was the old way of saying "good-bye," and is said to have been given to this plant because it dropped its petals as soon as it was picked.

Speirostachya (spi-ro-sta-ki-a). G. "Speiro" (to twist); "stachya" (a spike). Second bot. name.

Spergula (sper-gu-la). L. "Spargo" (to scatter); because the plant scatters its seeds widely. Bot. name Spurry group.

Spergularia (sper-gu-la-ri-a). L. adj., "like the Spergula." Second bot. name.

Sphacelata (sfas-e-la-ta). G. "Sphacelos" (gangrene); *i.e.*, withered, or having a dead sort of look.

Sphærica (sfer-i-ka). L. "Like a ball." Second bot. name.

Sphæro-Carpa (sfer-o-kar-pa). G. "Sphaira" (a sphere); "carpa" (fruit); *i.e.*, fruit is ball-shaped. Second bot. name.

Sphærocephalum (sfer-o-se-fal-um). G. "Sphaero" (a sphere); "cephalos" (a head); *i.e.*, round-headed. Second bot. name.

Sphondylium (sfon-dil-i-um). G. name for an insect that gave out an unpleasant odour, and was given to the Cow Parsnip because of its nasty smell. Second bot. name.

Spicant (spi-kant). L. "Spico" (furnished with spines). Second bot. name.

Spicata (spi-ka-ta). L. adj., "furnished with

spikes "; *i.e.*, the flowers grow in spikes. Second bot. name.

Spica-Venti (spi-ka-ven-ti). L. "Spica" (an ear); "venti" (of the wind); because the silky spikes shake in the wind. Second bot. name.

Spignel (spig-nel). Eng. name of Meum group; said to be a corruption of "spike nail."

Spikelet (spik-let). A botanical term for the small cluster of flowers seen in the Grasses.

Spikenard (spik-nard). Eng. name for Inula Conyza, which is called Ploughman Spikenard. Spikenard is "spike," an ear or spike of the "nard," an aromatic Indian grass.

Spindle-Tree. Eng. name for Evonymous group. The wood of the tree, being tough and hard, was much used for making spindles, hence the name.

Spinosa (spin-o-sa). L. adj., "full of spines," Second bot. name.

Spinosisima (spin-o-sis-im-a). L. adj., superlative of "spinosa"; *i.e.*, plant covered with spines. Second bot. name.

Spinulosum (spin-u-lo-sum). L. adj., "full of small spines." Second bot. name.

Spiræa (spi-re-a). G. name for Meadow Sweet. Bot. name of a group.

Spiranthes (spir-anth-es). G. "Speir" (twisted round); "anthus" (a flower); *i.e.*, flowers grow spirally up the stalk. Bot. name Lady's Tresses' group.

Spleen Wort. Eng. name for Asplenium group, and partial translation of its bot. name.

Sponhemica (spon-hem-i-ka). Second bot. name variety Cut-leaved Saxifrage.

Spruce (sproos). German. "Sprossen" (a sprout);

from the many short branchlets that are on the tree. Eng. name for Picea division of the Pines.

Spur. A botanical term, when the lower part of a petal has a hollow conical projection like the spur of a cock.

Spurge (spurj). A corruption of L. " expurgere "; refers to the medicinal properties of the plant. Eng. name of a group.

Spuria (spu-ri-a). L. adj., " not genuine." Second bot. name.

Spurry (spur-i). Old French " sporrie." Eng. name of Spergula group.

Squalidus (skwol-id-us). L. adj., " squalid." Second bot. name.

Squamaria (skwa-ma-ri-a). L. adj., " scaly "; refers to the fleshy scale that cover the rootstock. Second bot. name.

Squarrosus (skwar-ro-sus). L. adj., " rough or scurvy." Second bot. name.

Squill (skwil). Eng. rendering of G. " skilla " (name of the plant).

Squinancy Wort (skwin-an-se-wort). Eng. name of Asperula Cynanchia. " Squinancy " is nothing but a corruption of second bot. name " cynanchia."

Stachys (sta-kis). G. " Stachys " (a spike or ear of corn) ; refers to the general look of the flower. Bot. name of group.

Stagnalis (stag-na-lis). L. adj., " belonging to a pond." Second bot. name.

Stagnina (stag-ni-na). L. adj., " stagnant water "; refers to the plant doing well on boggy heaths. Second bot. name.

Star-of-Bethlehem. Eng. name for Ornithogalum, Umbeellatum. Gets its name because its white star-like flower resemble the pictures of the star that indicated the birth of the Saviour.

Star Wort. Eng. name for a group, and translation of its bot. name " Stellaria."

Statice (stat-i-se). G. name (from " statikos," to stop) for some plant having astringent qualities. Bot. name of a group.

Stellaria (stel-ar-i-a). L. adj., " star-like "; from the star-like look of the flowers. Bot. name Starwort group.

Stellatae (stel-a-te). L. " Stella " (a star). Bot. name of a family.

Stellatum (stel-a-tum). L. adj., " starry." Second bot. name.

Stellulata (stel-u-la-ta). L. " A little star." Second bot. name.

Stenoptera (sten-o-ter-a). G. " Stenos " (narrow); " pteron " (a wing); refers to the wings on the seeds of the plant. Second bot. name.

Sterilis (ster-i-lis). L. adj., " barren." Second bot. name.

Strictocarpa (stik-to-car-pa). G. " Striktos " (punc-tured); " carpa " (fruit). Second bot. name.

Stigma (stig-ma). A bot. term for the top of the style on which the fertilising pollen falls.

Stipularis (stip-ul-ar-is). L. adj., " having stipules."

Stipule (stip-ul). A bot. term for the small leaf or scale-like appendage at the base of leaf or stalk.

Stitch Wort. Eng. name for two or three of the Star-worts. Gets its name from having been thought to be an antidote for stitch in the side.

Stock (stok). Eng. name for Matthiola group.

Stolonifera (sto-lon-if-era). L. "Stolo" (a shoot); "fera" (a bearer); from its runners, which root. Second bot. name.

Stonecrop. Eng. name for Sedum group. Gets its name because, owing to fleshy leaves, the plant readily imbibes moisture, and so manages to live on stony walls.

Stramonium (stra-mo-ni-um). Formerly bot. name for Thorn Apple, but now used as its second bot. name.

Strapwort. Eng. name of a group, and translation of its bot. name "Corrigiola."

Stratiotes (strat-i-o-tez). G. adj., "pertaining to soldiers"; referring to the sword-shaped leaves of the plant. Bot. name of Water-Soldier group.

Strawberry. In the 10th century it was called Streow-berige, referring to its runners being like straw. Eng. name of Fragaria group.

Strawberry Tree. Eng. name for Arbutus Unedo; from shape of its fruit being like that of the Straw-berry.

Striatum (stri-a-tum). L. adj., "streaked"; referring to the fine parallel lines as groves or ridges. Second bot. name.

Stricta (strik-ta). L. adj., "growing upright." A common second bot. name applied to different plants of different families.

Strigosa (strig-o-sa). L. "Striga" (a row); *i.e.*, covered with rows of sharp rigid hairs. Second bot. name.

Strigulosa (strig-u-lo-sa). L. dim. of "strigosa"; *i.e.*, the hairs are small. Second bot. name.

Strumarium (stroo-ma-ri-um). L. "Strumus" was

the name of a plant that cured the "struma," a scrophulus tumour. An old name for Burweed.

Sturmia (stur-mi-a). Group name of some botanists for Liparis.

Style. Bot. name for the thin thread-like stalk, from the ovary, that carries the "stigma," the essential feature of the female flower.

Stylosa (stil-o-sa). L. adj., "full of styles." Second bot. name.

Suaeda (swe-da). Arabic name of plant. Bot. name of a group. The plants of this group secret soda taken from the soil.

Suberosa (su-ber-osa). L. adj., "corky," from "suber" (the cork tree). The bark of this Elm is more corky than that of the other Elms. Second bot. name for a variety of Common Elm.

Sub. L. "Under," but when used to form a compound word it has the meaning of "slightly, or somewhat like," whatever the other part of the word may mean.

Suberose (e-roz). L. "Slightly gnawed."

,, **caerulium** (se-ru-li-um). L. "Slightly blue."

,, **compressum** (com-pres-um). L. "Somewhat pressed."

,, **cordata** (kor-da-ta). L. "Somewhat heart shaped."

,, **cristata** (kris-ta-ta). L. "Somewhat crested."

,, **erectus** (e-rekt-us). L. "Somewhat erect."

,, **glabra** (gla-bra). L. "Somewhat smooth."

,, **globosa** (glo-bo-sa). L. "Somewhat ball-like."

,, **mersum** (mer-sum). L. "Under water."

,, **nuda** (nu-da). L. "Somewhat naked"; *i.e.*, without leaves or hairs.

,, **repens** (re-pens). L. "Somewhat creeping."

All of these are used as second bot. names.

Subterraneum (sub-te-ran-ne-im). L. adj., "underground"; because the seed, when ripe, turns downwards and sows itself in the ground. Second bot. name for Underground Clover.

Subtomentosum (sub-to-ment-o-sum). L. adj., "slightly covered with downy hairs." Second bot. name.

Subularia (su-bu-la-ri-a). L. "Subula" (an awl). Bot. name Awl Wort group.

Subulata (su-bu-la-ta). L. adj., "awl-like." Second bot. name.

Subverticillatus (sub-ver-ti-sil-a-tus). L. "Sub" and verticillatus" (a whorl); *i.e.*, imperfectly whorled.

Succisa (suk-sis-a). L. "Cut off"; refers to the root, which looks as if bitten off. Second bot. name Devil's bit.

Succisaefolia (suk-sis-e-fol-ia). L. "Succisa" and "folia" (leaves). Second bot. name.

Succory (suk-or-i). Another Eng. name for Chicory, and probably nothing more or less than a corruption of that name. Second bot. name.

Suecica (su-e-se-ka). Second bot. name Dwarf Cornel.

Suffocatum (suf-o-ka-tum). L. adj., "suffocated"; from the small flowers being crowded together on short stems, close to the ground. Second bot. name Suffocated Clover.

Suffruiticulosa (suf-ru-ti-kul-o-sa). L. adj., "somewhat shrubby." Second bot. name.

Sulcata (sul-ka-ta). L. adj., "furrowed." Second bot. name.

Sulphur Weed. Another Eng. name for Hog's Fennel; from sulphur-like colour of the flowers.

Sun Dew. Gets its Eng. name from the dew-like drops

of clammy fluid which exude from the leaves. Bot. name for Drossera group.

Supinum (su-pi-num). L. adj., "lying on the back." Second bot. name.

Surculosa (sur-kul-osa). L. adj., "full of suckers." Second bot. name.

Sycamore (sik-a-mor). A corruption of G. "suko-moros" (name of mulberry fig). Is Eng. name for Acer Pseudoplatanus.

Sylvaticus (sil-vat-i-kus). L. adj., "plants growing wild." A very common second bot. name applied to plants of various families.

Sylvestris (sil-ves-tris). L. adj., "living in woods or shady places." Second bot. name for many plants.

Sylvicola (sil-vi-ko-la). L. "Sylva" (a wood); "cola" (a dweller in). Second bot. name.

Symphytum (sim-fi-tum). G. "Symphyo" (to unite); from the healing properties of the plant. Bot. name for Comfrey group.

Systyla (sis-til-a). G. "Syn" (together); "stylos" (a style); *i.e.*, united. Second bot. name.

T

Tabernaemontani (ta-ber-ne-mon-tan-i). "Mount Tabor" in L. dress. Second bot. name.

Tamarix (tam-ar-iks). Hebrew. "Tamarik" (that which has a cleansing property); *i.e.*, purifies the blood. Bot. name Tamarisc group.

Tamus (tam-us). L. name for the plant. Bot. name Black Bryony group.

Tanacetum (tan-a-se-tum). G. Corruption of "atha-naon" (everlasting). Bot. name for Tansy group.

Tansy. Eng. name for Tanacetum group. Probably a corruption and contraction of the L. "Tanacetum."

Taraxacum (tar-aks-a-kum). G. "Tarasso" (to change); from the effects of the plant on the blood. Bot. name Dandelion group.

Taraxci (tar-aks-se). L. adj., "taraxacum-like." Second bot. name.

Taraxcifolia (tar-aks-i-fol-ia). L. "Taraxacum" and "folia" (leaves); from the leaves of the plant being like those of the Dandelion. Second bot. name.

Tare. An Eng. name for the Hairy Vetch.

Tarragon (tar-a-gon). Persian. "Tarkum" (dragon wort). Is the cultivated species of Artemissia group.

Taxifolia (tak-si-fol-ia). L. "Taxus" and "folia" (leaves); the leaf of the plant being like that of the Yew. Second bot. name.

Taxus (tak-sus). G. "Taxos" (a bow); the wood of the Yew was much used for bows. Bot. name Yew group.

Teasel (tez-l). Dutch. "Teesen" (to pick or pull about). Eng. name for Dipsacus group, because the prickly head or bur of the plant is used to raise nap on cloth.

Teesdalia (tez-dal-ia). After Teesdale, a Yorkshire botanist, died 1804. Bot. name of a group.

Tectorum (tek-tor-um). L. adj., "on roofs"; where it is often found growing. Second bot. name.

Telephium (tele-fium). L. After Telephus, son of Hercules, King of Mysia. Second bot. name.

Telmatia (tel-ma-ti-a). G. " Of a marsh "; where the plant often grows. Second bot. name.

Temulentum (tem-u-len-tum).

Temulum (tem-u-lum). Both L. adj., " drunken "; from the drunken jerky way the flowers nod. Second bot. names.

Tenella (ten-el-a). L. adj., " somewhat tender." Second bot. name.

Tenuis (te-new-is). L. adj., " thin, slender, narrow."

Tenuior (te-new-or). L. adj. comparative of " tenuis."

Tenuissimum (te-new-is-i-mum). L. adj. superlative of " tenuis."

All three used as second bot. name for some plant.

Tenuiflorus (te-new-i-flo-rus). L. " Tenuis " and " florus " (a flower); slender flowered. Second bot. name.

Tenuifolia (te-new-fol-ia). L. " Tenuis " and " folia " (leaves); thin leaved. Second bot. name.

Tenuisecta (te-new-sek-ta). L. " Tenuis " and " secta " (cut); the leaf segments being very fine and thin. Second bot. name. -

Tephrosanthos (tef-ro-san-thos). G. " Tephro " (ashes); " anthos " (a flower); from the ash-like colour of the flower. Second bot. name.

Teretiscula (ter-et-is-ku-la). L. " Teres " (round); " culus " (a dim. suffix corresponding to Eng. " ish "); *i.e.*, roundish. Second bot. name.

Teretifolium (ter-et-i-fol-i-um). L. " Teres " (round); " folium " (a leaf); round-leaved. Second bot. name.

Terrestre (te-res-tre). L. adj., " of the land." Second bot. name.

Tetrandrum (tet-ran-drum). G. " Tetera " (four);

"andros" (a man); *i.e.*, plant has four male
flowers. Second bot. name.

Tetragonum (tet-ra-go-num). G. "Tetra" (four);
"gonum" (angles); *i.e.*, four-sided. Second bot.
name.

Tetrahit (tet-ra-hit). G. "Tetra" (four); "hit"
(sided). Second bot. name.

Tetralix (tet-ra-liks). G. "Tetra" (four); "lix"
(crossways). Second bot. name.

Tetraphyllum (tet-ra-fil-um). G. "Tetra" (four);
"phyllum" (a leaf). Second bot. name.

Tetrapla (tet-ra-pla). G. "Fourfold." Second bot.
name.

Tetrapteron (tet-ra-ter-on). G. "Tetra" (four);
"pteron" (wings). Second bot. name.

Tetrasperma (tet-ra-sper-ma). G. "Four-seeded."

Teucrium (tew-kri-um). After Teucer, King of Troy,
who first used the plant in medicine. Bot. name of
a group.

Thalecress (tha-le-cress). Eng. name for Wall Cress
(see Thaliana).

Thaliana (tha-li-a-na). After Thalia, one of the Muses,
who presided over festivals. Second bot. name
Wall Cress.

Thalictrum (tha-lik-trum). G. "Thallo" (to flourish).
Bot. name of a group.

Thapsiforma (thap-si-for-ma). L. "Thapsus" and
"forma" (shaped). Second bot. name.

Thapsus (thap-sus). L. After the name of a place in
Africa, where the plant grew abundantly. Herbalists' old name for the Mullein. Second bot.
name Great Mullein.

Thesium (the-si-um). After Theseus, King of Athens, B.C. 1235. Bot. name of a group.

Thelypteris (the-li-ter-is). G. "Thelys" (a female); "pteris" (a fern). Second bot. name.

Thistle. A.S. "Thistel." Eng. name for Carduus group.

Thlaspi (thlas-pi). G. "Thlao" (flatten); from the flattened look of the seeds. Bot. name Pennycress group.

Thorn Apple. Eng. name for Datura plant. Gets "apple" from the shape of the fruit; "thorn" from the many prickles which cover the fruit.

Thrift. Eng. name for Armeria group.

Thrincia (thrin-si-a). G. "Thrincos" (a battlement); from the look of the crown on the pod. A synonym for Leontodon, used by some botanists.

Throw Wax. Another Eng. name for Hare's Ear.

Thyme (tim). Eng. name for Thymus group.

Thymeleaceæ (thy-mel-a-se-e). G. "Thymelaia" (a name for the Daphne); and "aceous" (like). Bot. name for Daphne family.

Thymus (thy-mus). G. "The soul or heart," was the name for Thyme because its balsamic odours strengthened animal spirits. Bot. name for a group.

Thyrsiflora (ther-si-flo-ra). L. adj., "thrysus-shaped flowers." Thrysus is a botanical term for a particular sort of flowering; *i.e.*, when the middle part of a bunch of flowers has its flowers on longer stalks than those above or below. Second bot. name Tufted Lysimachia.

Thyrysoideus (ther-soi-deus). L. adj., "thrysus-like" (see Thyrsiflora). Second bot. name.

Tilia (til-i-a). L. name for the Lime. Bot. name for Lime group.

Tiliaceæ (til-i-a-se-e). L. "Tilia" and "aceous" (like). Bot. name for Lime family.

Tillaea (til-la-e). After Tilli, Italian botanist, died 1740. Bot. name of a group.

Timothy Grass. Eng. name for one of the grasses Phleum. Said to have received the name Timothy in America.

Tinctoria (tingk-tor-ia). L. adj., "used for dyeing." Second bot. name.

Tinea (tin-e-a). L. "A moth" (see Neo-tinea). Was an old botanical name for some of the Orchids.

Toadflax. This name is the outcome of two mistakes. The L. name for the plant was "bubonium," but mistakenly was written "bufonium." Now "bufo" is L. for a Toad. The group to which the plant belongs has nothing to do with Flax, but the name "linaria" was given it because the leaves of the plants of this group were like those belonging to the "Linum" (flax) group. Eng. name for Linaria Vulgaris.

Tofielda (to-field-a). After Tofield, a Yorkshire botanist. Bot. name of a group.

Tomentosa (to-ment-o-sa). L. "Tomentum" (stuffing for cushions); *i.e.*, downy. Second bot. name.

Tooth Wort. Gets this name from the roots of the plant being thought to be like human teeth. Eng. name for Lathraea group.

Tordylium (tor-dil-i-um). G. name of plant. Bot. name of a group.

Torilis (tor-il-is). G. "Toreo" (to emboss); from the

look of the fruit. Was once group name for the
Hedge Parsley.

Tormentilla (tor-men-til-a). From the French for
"colic," for which the root of the plant was used.
Second bot. name.

Torminalis (tor-men-al-is). L. "Tormina" (colic);
the fruit of the tree was used as a remedy. Second
bot. name Wild Service Tree.

Touch-Me-Not. Eng. name for Yellow Balsam, and
translation of its second bot. name "Noli-me-
tangere."

Tower Cress. Eng. name for one of the Rock Cress
group. "Tower" is a translation of its second
bot. name Turrita.

Tower Mustard. Eng. name for Arabis Perfoliata.
Although its group. name is now Arabis, when
named by Linneus its group name was "Turrites,"
i.e., "Tower," and thus in its Eng. name its old
group name still lives..

Trachelium (tra-ki-li-um). G. "Trachelos" (the.
throat); the plant was used for inflammation of the
throat. Second bot. name.

Trachyodon (tra-ki-o-don). G. "Trachia" (the wind-
pipe); "odon" (a tooth); from the tooth-like
edging of the sheath. Second bot. name.

Treacle Mustard. Eng. name for Erysimum Cheiranthoides. The word Treacle has nothing to do with
Molasses or Golden Syrup. There was a sovereign
remedy against all poisons, and called G.
"theriakos." This plant was one of the ingredients; it also had some "little beasts," G.
"theriakel." Treacle is a corruption of that word.

Tragopogon (trag-o-po-gon). G. "Tragos" (a goat);

15

" pogon " (a beard); from the hairy beard-like look
the plant has when its seed has ripened. Bot. name
for Salsify group.

Trefoil. Eng. rendering of L. " trifolium."

Tremula (trem-u-la). L. adj., " shaking "; from the
constant movement of the leaf.

Tri and Tres. G. or L. When used as a prefix means
three.

Triandra (tri-an-dra). G. " Tri " (three); " andra "
(males); i.e., flower has three equal stamens.
Second bot. name.

Triangularis (tri-ang-u-la-ris). L. " Three-angled."
Second bot. name.

Trichomanes (tri-kom-an-es). G. " A growth of hair
or bristle "; refers to a bristle which grows out
of the seed vessel; from this it gets both its Eng.
and bot. names. Bot. name of Bristle group.

Trichonema (tri-ko-ne-ma). G. " Trichos " (hair);
" nema " (a filament); i.e., hair-like filament. In
former edition of Bentham and Hooker this was
the group name for Romulea group.

Trichoides (trik-oi-des). G. " Trichos " (hair);
" oides " (like). Second bot. name.

Trichophyllus (trik-o-fil-us). G. " Trichos " (hair);
" phyllus " (a leaf); i.e., hair-like leaf. All leaves
growing under water have a tendency to grow hair-
like, so as to get the elements necessary for the
plant.

Tricolour (tri-co-lor). L. adj., " three-coloured," which
the flower has. Second bot. name of Heartsease.

Tricornus (tri-kor-nus). L. " Three-horned "; from
" cornus " (a horn). Second bot. name.

Tricostata (tri-kos-ta-ta). L. adj., "three-ribbed"; from "costa" (a rib). Second bot. name.

Tridactylites (tri-dak-til-i-tes). L. adj., "three-fingered"; from "dactylus" (a finger). Second bot. name.

Tridentatum (tri-den-ta-tum). L. adj., "three-toothed"; from "dens" (a tooth). Second bot. name.

Trientale (tri-en-tal). Eng. rendering of Trientalis.

Trientalis (tri-en-tal-is). L. adj., "containing one-third of a foot"; *i.e.*, four inches, which is the average height of the plant. Bot. name of a group.

Trifolium (tri-fol-i-um). L. adj., "three-leaved"; the usual number of leaflets into which the leaf is divided. Bot. name of Clover group.

Trifoliata (tri-fol-i-ata). L. adj., "three-leaved." Second bot. name.

Triflora (tri-flo-ra). L. adj., "three-flowered." Second bot. name.

Trifidus (tri-fi-dus). L. adj., "three-cleft"; from "fidus." (a cleft). Second bot. name.

Triglochin (tri-glo-kin). G. adj., "three-barbed or pointed"; refers to the fruit when ripe separating into three points. Bot. name Arrow-grass group.

Triglumis (tri-glu-mis). L. "Three" and "gluma" (a husk); *i.e.*, three-husked. Second bot. name.

Trigonel (tri-go-nel). Eng. rendering of Trigonella.

Trigonella (tri-go-nel-la). G. "Three"; "gonia" (angles); "ella" (dim); *i.e.*, little; from the somewhat triangular shape of the flower. Bot. name of a group.

Trigranulata (tri-gran-u-la-ta). L. adj., "having three

little knobs "; from "granulatus " (a little knob or tubercule). Second bot. name.

Trigynum (tri-jin-um). G. " Three "; " gune " (a woman); there being three females in the flower. Second bot. name.

Trinervis (tri-ner-vis). L. adj., " three-nerved "; refers to three distinct nerves in the leaf. Second bot. name.

Trinia (trin-ia). After Trinius, a German botanist, who died 1844. Bot. name for a group.

Triodia (tri-o-dia). G. adj., " three-toothed "; from " odos " (a tooth); refers to three very small teeth at the top of the husk of the seed. Bot. name of a group.

Tripartita (tri-par-ti-ta). L. adj., " three-cleft "; refers to the three lobes into which the leaf is divided. Second bot. name.

Tripetla (tri-pet-la). L. adj., " three-petaled "; refers to the number on the flower. Second bot. name.

Tripolium (tri-po-li-um). G. " Three " and "-polium " (changes); because the flower changes its colour three times in the day. Second bot. name.

Triphyllos (tri-fil-los). G. adj., " three-leaved "; because of the number of the lobes of the leaf. Second bot. name.

Triquetrum (tri-kwet-rum). L. adj., " three-cornered "; refers to the shape of the stem. Second bot. name.

Trisetum (tri-se-tum). L. adj., " thrice-bristled "; refers to the hair-like stiff awns. Group name used by some botanists instead of Avena for the Yellow Oat.

Trisulca (tri-sul-ka). L. adj., " thrice-furrowed." Second bot. name.

Triticum (trit-i-kum). L. name for wheat; from " tritus " (ground to flour). Group name used by some botanists instead of Agropyrum for Couch Grass.

Trivial. The " trivial " name of a plant is its second bot. name, and is given by way of distinguishing it from the plants belonging to the same group. The same " trivial " name may be and is given to many different plants, provided in each case the plant so named belongs to a different group; but in no case can the same " trivial " name be given to two different plants in the same group.

Trivialis (triv-i-al-is). L. adj., "trivial or common." Second bot. name.

Trollius (trol-li-us). Old German. " Troll " (a globe); from the shape of the flower being globe-like. Bot. name of a group.

Truncata (trung-ka-ta). L. adj., "shortened," as if the ends had been cut off; refers to the look of the leaves. Second bot. name.

Tuberculatus (tu-ber-ku-la-tus). L. adj., "covered with small knobby lumps." Second bot. name.

Tuberosus (tu-ber-o-sus). L. adj., " full of tubers." A common second bot. name applied to many different plants.

Tulipa (tu-li-pa). A corruption of the Persian word "tolibum " (turban); because of a fancied resemblance in the shape of the flower to a turban. Bot. name of Tulip group.

Tunbridgense (tun-brij-en-se). " Tunbridge " in Latin dress. Second bot. name.

Tunica (tu-nik-a). L. for " under-garment "; applied to the skin of a seed or coat of a bulb.

Turnip. A compound word of " tur " (round) and

"naepe" (the Saxon name for the plant). Eng. name for the cultivated varieties of Brassica, Napus.

Turrita (tur-ri-ta). L. "Turris" (a tower); refers to the tower-like look of the flower. Second bot. name.

Turritis (tur-ri-tis). See Tower Mustard.

Tussilago (tus-i-la-go). L. "Tussis" (a cough); for which the plant was used as a remedy. Bot. name Coltsfoot group.

Tutsan (tut-san). French. "Tout-sain" (all heal); from its being of use in stopping bleeding. Second bot. name for one of the Hypericum group.

Twayblade (twa-blad). "Tway" (an old form of "two.") and "blade" (leaves). Eng. name for one of Orchid groups.

Typha (ti-fa). G. "Tuphos" (a marshy pool); where the plant is found. Bot. name Reedmace group.

Typhaceæ (ti-fa-se-e). G. "Typha" and "aceous" (like). Bot. name of a family.

U

Ulex (u-leks). Celtic. "Uile" (all); "ex" (prickle). Bot. name Furze group.

Uliginosum (u-lij-in-o-sum). L. adj., "full of moisture"; *i.e.*, a marsh; where the plant loves to grow. A common second bot. name for many plants.

Ulmaceæ (ul-ma-se-e). L. "Ulmus" (the elm tree); "aceous" (like). Bot. name of a family.

Ulmaria (ul-ma-ri-a). L. "Ulmus" (elm); the leaf being like that of the Elm. At one time

"Ulmaria" was the common name for Meadow
Sweet. Now it is used as its second bot. name.

Ulmifolius (ul-mi-fol-ius). L. "Ulmus" and "folius"
(a leaf); *i.e.*, from the leaf being like that of the
Elm. Second bot. name.

Ulmus (ul-mus). L. name for Elm. Bot. name Elm
group.

Umbellate (um-bel-at). Eng. name for Umbelliferae
family.

Umbellatum (um-bel-a-tum). L. "Umbella" (a little
shadow); hence a sunshade or parasol. Second
bot. name for one or two plants, from some characteristic they happen to have in common with those
plants of the Umbellate family.

Umbelliferæ (um-bel-if-er-e). L. "Umbella" (a small
shadow); "ferro." (to carry). Bot. name for Umbellate family. There are a large number of
flowers, mostly white, which at the end of the main
flowering stalk break into a number of clusters of
flowers, each having a separate stalk of its own.
Each of these is an "umbel." The length of the
stalk of each umbel varies according to where it
springs from the main stalk; but the general result
is that all the clusters are in the same flat plane, and
the whole lot together is viewed as the "flower."

Umbilicus (um-bil-i-kus). L. adj., "pertaining to the
navel." Second bot. name.

Umbrosum (um-bro-sum). L. adj., "grows in shady
places." A common second bot. name for many
plants.

Undulatum (un-du-la-tum). L. adj., "wavy." Second
bot. name.

Unedo (un-ed-o). L. name for the tree. Pliny tells us

it was called " Unedo " from "un ", (once only)
"edo " (eaten); because of the nasty taste of the
fruit. Second bot. name for Strawberry tree.

Unicinella (un-i-se-nel-a).   L. dim. of "uncinus" (a
small barb). Second bot. name.

Uniflora (un-i-flo-ra). L. adj., " one-flowered." Second
bot. name.

Uniglumis (un-i-glu-mis). L. "Uni" (one); " glumis "
(husk). Second bot. name.

Unilaterale (un-i-lat-er-ale). L. " Uni " (one); " later-
ale " (sided). Second bot. name.

Uralensis (u-ral-en-sis). The " Ural " mountains in
L. dress. Second bot. name.

Urbanum (ur-ban-um).

Urbicum (ur-bi-kum). Both. L. adj., " in the towns ";
where the plants are sometimes found. Second
bot. name.

Urens (u-rens). L. " Uro " (burning); i.e., stinging
like a nettle. Second bot. name.

Urtica (ur-ti-ka). L. " Uro " (burning); from the
sensation caused by the sting. Bot. name Nettle
group.

Urticaceæ (ur-ti-ka-se-e). L. " Urtica " and " aceous "
(like). Bot. name for Nettle family.

Ursinum (ur-si-num). L. " Bearish "; i.e., rough.
Second bot. name.

Usitatissimum (u-si-ta-tis-si-mum). L. adj., superlative of " most common." Second bot. name.

Ustulata (us-tu-la-ta). L. adj., " scorched "; from the
burnt-like look of the buds. Second bot. name.

Utricularia (u-tri-ku-la-ria). L. " Utriculus " (a small
bladder); from the many small bladders on the
plant. Bot. name of Bladder Wort group.

Uva-Crispa (u-va-kris-pa). L. "Uva" (a bunch of any fruit); "crispa" (curled). Second bot. name of Wild Gooseberry.

Uva-Ursi (u-va-ur-si). L. "Uva" (a bunch of any fruit); "ursi" (of the bear). Second bot. name Common Bearberry.

V

Vaccinium (vak-si-ni-um). L. A corruption of "bacca" (a berry); from the plant bearing many berries. Bot. name Heath group.

Vaciniifolia (va-si-ni-fol-ia). L. "Vacinium" and "folia" (leaves); from the leaf being like that of the Vacinium. Second bot. name.

Vagans, (vag-ans). L. adj., "wandering." Second bot. name.

Vaginatum (va-ji-na-tum). L. "Vagina" (a sheath). Second bot. name.

Vaillantii (vail-lan-ti). After Vaillantii. Second bot. name.

Valerandi (val-er-and-i). After Valerand. Second bot. name Brookweed.

Valerian (va-le-ri-an). Eng. rendering of Valeriana.

Valeriana (va-le-ri-an-a). L. "Valeo" (to be powerful); from its medicinal effects. Bot. name Valerian group.

Valerianeæ (va-le-ri-a-ne-e). L. Bot. name Valerian family.

Valerianella (va-le-ri-a-nel-a). L. dim. of Valerian. Bot. name Cornsalad group.

Variabilis (va-ri-ab-il-is). L. adj., "changeable." Second bot. name.

Varians (va-ri-ans). L. adj., "varying." Second bot. name.

Variegatum (va-ri-e-gat-um). L. adj., "variegated." Second bot. name.

Velutinus (vel-u-ti-nus). L. adj., "velvety"; from its coating of fine hairs. Second bot. name.

Veneris (ve-ner-is). See Capillus-Veneris.

Venulosa (ven-u-lo-sa). L. adj., "full of veins." Second bot. name.

Venus'-Comb. Is another name for Shepherd's Needle. According to Folkhard, in early days of the Christian Church the monks dedicated many plants to Our Lady the Virgin Mary, but in Puritan times it was put into Venus' Comb.

Verbascum (ver-bas-cum). L. Corruption of "barbascum" (bearded); from the shaggy look of the foliage. Bot. name Mullein group.

Verbena (ver-be-na). L. word for the "sacred branches" of olive, laurel, or myrtle. Bot. name Vervein group.

Verbenaceæ (ver-be-na-si-e). L. "Verbena" and "aceous" (like). Bot. name Vervein family.

Verbenaca (ver-be-na-ka). L. adj., "like the Vervena." Second bot. name for the Wild Sage.

Veris (ver-is).

Verna (ver-na).

Vernalis (ver-na-lis). All three L. adj. from "ver" (spring). Used as second bot. name, and applied to many different plants.

Veronica (ver-on-i-ka). After St. Veronica, because the impression left on her veil after she had used it to wipe the Saviour's brow resembles the look of the flower. Bot. name Speedwell group.

Verrucosa (ve-ru-ko-sa). L. adj., "full of warts"; from "verruca" (a wart). Second bot. name.

Versifolia (ver-si-fol-ia). L. "Versus" (changeable); "folia" (leaves). Second bot. name.

Versicolor (ver-si-co-lor). L. "Versus" (changeable); "color" (colour). Second bot. name.

Verticillatum (ver-ti-sil-a-tum). L. "The whirl of a spindle"; *i.e.*, arranged around the stalk in a ring. Second bot. name.

Vervein (ver-van). Celtic. "Ferfain." At one time called Holy Herb, and much prized by the Druids. Eng. name for Verbena group.

Verum (ver-um). L. adj., "genuine." Second bot. name.

Vesca (ves-ka). L. adj., "small or feeble." Second bot. name.

Vesicaria (ve-si-ka-ri-a). L. "Vesica" (a bladder); the seed being somewhat bladder-like in shape. Second bot. name.

Vespertina (ves-per-ti-na). L. adj., "at eventide"; when the flower blooms. Second bot. name.

Vestitus (ves-ti-tus). L. adj., "clothed." Second bot. name.

Vetch (vech). Derivation obscure. In Middle Ages the word was "fitch." Eng. name for Vicia group.

Vetchling (vech-ling). Eng. dim. of Vetch. Name given to two members of Pea group.

Viburnum (vi-bur-num). L. name for Wayfaring tree. Bot. name of a group.

Vicia (vik-ia). One derivation from L. "vincio" (to bind). Another from Celtic "gwig." Bot. name for Vetch group.

Viciaefolia (vik-i-fol-ia). L. " Vicia " and "folia " (leaves). A second bot. name of some botanists for Common Sainfoin.

Villarsia (vil-lars-ia). After Villers, a French botanist. Was Linneus' group name for Limnantheum.

Villicaulis (vil-i-kaw-lis). L. " Villi " (long weak hairs); " caulis " (a stem). Second bot. name.

Villosum (vil-o-sum). L. adj., " full of villi "; *i.e.*, long weak hair. Second bot. name.

Viminalis (vi-min-al-is). L. adj., " pertaining to osiers "; from " vimen " (a long pliant twig). Second bot. name.

Vinacea (vin-a-se-a). L. " Vinum " (wine); " aceous " (like); *i.e.*, wine colour or purplish red. Second bot. name.

Vinca (ving-ka). L. name of plant, from " Vincio " (to bind). Bot. name Periwinkle group.

Vineale (vin-e-al-e). L. adj., " belonging to the vine-yard "; because the plant is often there found. Second bot. name.

Viola (vi-o-la). L. name of plant. Bot. name Violet group.

Violaceæ (vi-ola-se-e). L. " Viola " and " aceous " (like). Bot. name Violet family.

Viper's Bugloss. " Viper's " is only a translation of " Echium," the group name of the plant (which see).

Virens (vi-rens). L. adj., " green and strong." Second bot. name.

Virga-Aurea (vir-ga-awr-ea). L. " Virga " (a twig); " aurea " (golden). Second bot. name of Golden-Rod.

Virgatum (vir-ga-tum). L. adj., "twiggy"; from "virga" (a twig). Second bot. name.

Viridis (vir-id-is). L. adj., "green." Second bot. name for several plants.

Viridiflora (vir-id-i-flo-ra). L. "Viridi" (green); "flora" (flowers). Second bot. name.

Virosa (vir-o-sa). L. adj., "having a bad smell." Second bot. name.

Viscosus (vis-ko-sus).

Viscaria (vis-ka-ri-a). Both L. adj., "sticky"; like birdlime. Second bot. name given to several plants.

Viscum (vis-kum). L. for Mistletoe, and also for bird-lime prepared from it. Bot. name Mistletoe group.

Vitalba (vit-al-ba). L. "Vit" (a vine); "alba" (white). Second bot. name for Travellers' Joy.

Vitellina (vi-teli-na). L. "Vitellus" (the yoke of an egg); because of the bright yellow colour of the branches. Second bot. name of Golden Osier.

Vitilis (vi-til-is). L. adj., "plaited." Second-bot. name.

Vitis-Idaea (vi-tis-i-de-a). L. adj., "vitis" (a vine of Idaea, a mountain of Asia Minor). Second bot. name Red Whortleberry.

Viviparum (vi-vip-ar-um). L. adj., "producing young alive); *i.e.*, produces buds while still attached to parent. Second bot. name.

Vulgaris (vul-gar-is). L. adj., "common." The most common of all second bot. names.

Vulgatum (vul-ga-tum). L. adj., "generally known." Second bot. name.

Vulneraria (vul-ne-ra-ri-a). L. adj., "belonging to wounds." Second bot. name.

Vulpia (vul-pi-a). L. "Vulpus" (a fox). Bot. name of a group used by some botanists instead of Fescue.

Vulpina (vul-pi-na). L. "Vulpus" (a fox); refers to colour. Second bot. name.

Vulvaria (vul-va-ri-a). L. "Volva" (a wrapper). Second bot. name Stinking Goosefoot.

W

Weld. Said to be derived from Spanish "qualda." Eng. name for Reseda Luteolais.

Whin. Welsh. "Cwyn" (a weed). Eng. name for the Ulex.

Whortleberry (whor-tl-beri). A.S. "Heoruthberge"; *i.e.*, heather berry. Eng. name for Vaccinium Myrtillus.

Willow. Welsh. "Gwial" (twigs). Eng. name for Salix group.

Winter Green. Eng. name Pyrola group.

Woad (wod). A.S. "Waad." Eng. name for Isatis group.

Woodrush. Eng. name of Luzula group.

Woodsia (woods-ia). After Joseph Woods, Eng. botanist, died 1864. Bot. name of a group.

Wormwood. A.S. "Werian" (to protect); "mod" (the mind); *i.e.*, mind-protector; from its medicinal properties. Eng. name for Artemisia Absinthium.

Wolffia. Bot. name for a sub-group of the Lemna group, and so called after J. F. Wolff, who, in 1801, published a work on the Lemna group.

Wallflower. Eng. name for Cheiranthus group. The

"Wall" of the name comes, it is said, from the
plant growing on walls, but so do other plants. In
1597 Gerarde called it "wallgilloflower," but in the
14th century the plant was called "violaria," and
the flowers were known as "viola" and "wal-
fair." Mark that there is only one "l" in "wal-
fair." The plant is a native of Southern Europe,
and was introduced into this country by the monks
of old. In those days "wal" meant "foreign"
(see Walnut), *i.e.*, foreign nut, which to this day
is fortunately only spelt with one "l." It therefore
looks as if the flower was first called "Walflower,"
i.e., foreign flower. Somehow a second "l" was
put in. "Wall" displaced "foreign," and a
wrong derivation for the word had to be found.
In this connection see Cheiranthus, the second bot.
name for Wallflower.

Watercress. Gets its "water" from where it is
generally found growing. Eng. name for Nasturtium group.

Wintercress. Eng. name for Barbarea group.

Water Lily. Eng. name for Nymphaeceæ family.

Water Soldier. Eng. name for a group, and translation
of its bot. name Stratiotes.

X

Xanthium (zan-thi-um). G. "Xanthos" (yellow).
Bot. name Burweed group.

Xylosteum (zi-los-ti-um). G. adj. "woody." Second
bot. name Fly Honeysuckle.

Y

Yam. West Indian. " Ihame " (name of tuber). Eng. name for Dioscorideae family.

Yarrow (yar-o). A.S. " Gearuwe." Eng. name for Achillea Millefolium.

Yew. A.S. " Iw." Eng. name for Taxus group.

Z

Zannichellia. After Zannichelli, a Venetian botanist, died 1729. Bot. name Horned Pondweed group.

Zostera (zos-ter-a). G. " Zoster " (a ribbon). Bot. name Grass-wrack group.

Zosterifolius (zos-ter-if-ol-i-us). G. " Zoster " and " folius " (a leaf). Second bot. name for Acute Pondweed.

Printed in Great Britain by Ebenezer Baylis & Son, The Trinity, Worcester

Lightning Source UK Ltd.
Milton Keynes UK
UKHW010635041021
391643UK00004B/154